GOD STORIES

GOD STORIES

They're So Amazing,
Only God Could
Make Them Happen

DONNA I. DOUGLAS

P.O. Box 4123, Lancaster, Pennsylvania 17604

To schedule author appearances, write: Author Appearances, Starburst Promotions, P.O. Box 4123, Lancaster, Pennsylvania 17604 or call (717) 293-0939. Website: www.starburstpublishers.com.

CREDITS:
Cover design by Richmond & Williams
Text design and composition by John Reinhardt Book Design

All scripture was taken from the New King James Version unless otherwise indicated.

GOD STORIES
Copyright © 1999 by Donna I. Douglas
All rights reserved

First Printing, July, 1999

ISBN: 1-892016-11-7
Library of Congress Catalog Number: 99-63783
Printed in the United States of America

*This book is dedicated to C. Mae Douglas,
the best mom on the planet!*

Love and kisses to your face,

D

"God is great, and therefore he will be sought: he is good, and therefore he will be found."

— JOHN JAY (1745–1829), FIRST CHIEF JUSTICE
OF THE U. S. SUPREME COURT

CONTENTS

CONTENTS

CONTENTS

ACKNOWLEDGMENTS

I WANT TO THANK EACH CONTRIBUTOR for his or her generosity of time and word. May you be blessed abundantly for your willingness to be a part of this project.

I would like to thank all of the people who helped me gather phone numbers, make phone calls, and send faxes and emails in order to line up the interviews: Paula Waterhouse, Mary Clement, Sarah Dowdy, Cynthia Calhoun, Kim Guenther, Judith Service Montier, Eric Smith, Sandra Bell, Lisa Foster, Ollie E. Brown, Aimee Birdwell, Michele Clark Jenkins, Zoro, Frank D'Amato, Dennis and Anita Tinerino, Tim Stone, Jennifer Kemp Andrews, Dak, Claudio, and Richard Burkhart.

Mary Clement: for your editing skills and for being as happy for me when Houston's has wild mushroom soup as I am for you when it snows.

I would like to thank my friend, music attorney, and biggest cheerleader, James Randolph Smith. You know I'm the president of your fan club.

To my manager, Stan Bernstein: You are my gift from God. Thank you for your wisdom and guidance. Your belief in me gives me wings.

To Sharon and Dave Robie, Heather Stroobosscher, Chad Allen, and Peg Couch: Thank you for all your encouragement and for the vision to make *God Stories* happen.

To my family: Mommy, Di and Dave, Rick, Darlene, Erika (let's go swim with dolphin, Lem) and Austin (grrrrrrh!), aunts, uncles, and cousins galore. You're the best . . . I wish Granny and Dad could have been here to see this happen.

To Winnie, Abi, Kymbee, Alexis, Cody, Denver, Jermaine, Torrye, Nathan and Olivia, Jon-Michael, Sean, Nick, Will, Matt, Courtney, Desi, Amber, Olivia, Jason, Rebecca, Lawton, Will, Chazzy, Jerry, Chris, Mikey, Ashley, Amanda, and anyone else who calls me Auntie D: You light up my world and bring me tremendous joy. I love seeing life through your eyes.

To my "sista" girlies: Thanks for all the prayers, the listening endurance, the magnitude of laughter, and of course . . . the ladies' luncheons and triple lattes.

To my brother-boys: for the movie marathons, the laughter, and the drives at sunset to clear the cobwebs. You're the best!

To my Bible mentors, Patsy and Al Rhodes, for letting me ask you every question about spiritual matters that has ever popped into my head without ever sending me home or suggesting I find other mentors. I love you.

To my many wonderful teachers: Mrs. Ellington (4th grade), Mrs. Hatton (6th grade), Mrs. Whipple (12th grade English), Janet Rodgers (piano instructor), Ms. Peggy Barber (director of *Singers*), Dr. Strozier (English 101), Val Barnes "Ba-narnes" (greatest chaperone on all the Singers tours!), Maggie B for the lessons on the laptop, and Debi Ladd (Joyce Meyer Junior)—buy a date book and go on the road!

To my pastor, John Fichtner, Beth, Mark, Debi, John, Angie, Lance, Debi, and my Liberty Church family in Marietta, Georgia: Thank you for not just telling me but for showing me what the joy of the Lord and being clothed in humility look like and for constantly and consistently demonstrating the unconditional love, mercy, and grace of God. Becoming a part of your fellowship has allowed me to experience a little slice of heaven on earth.

INTRODUCTION

E VERY DAY, ALL AROUND US there is indisputable evidence
of God's love, power, and presence in our lives. In ways that
are both miraculous and commonplace, He intervenes to reveal
Himself.

After many intimate experiences in my own life, which I could
only attribute to supernatural encounters with God Himself, I
began referring to these events as *God Stories*. As I shared my
God Stories with those around me, I was taken aback at how
often people responded by telling me their own God Stories. My
surprise quickly turned to excitement and one thing led to another until one day I found myself writing the book you are now
holding.

In addition to a number of my own stories, I interviewed over
fifty celebrities and included theirs as well. These stories are about
all kinds of different people: singers, actors, authors, politicians,
sports figures, and people of prominence from the business world.
Some of these people I had met before; others I had the pleasure
of meeting for the first time. I was introduced to many through
mutual acquaintances and others I contacted through agents,
managers, and publicists. Each story begins with biographical
details about the contributor and interesting information about
the interview.

The unveiling of these amazing occurrences in our lives seems
to become manifest with more frequency as we become more
adept at developing the ability to notice. Whether it be through
the first cry of a newborn baby, a tumor that has mysteriously
disappeared, the multicolored magnificence of a sunset, an unexpected job promotion, seeing an impossible situation brought

to order, or the simple embrace of someone you love—everywhere we turn, God's personal and interactive participation in our lives is undeniable.

We can be assured that in everything God is in control and that He not only sees the big picture, He painted it. He has a plan and a purpose for each of us. Before He ever hung the first star, He knew of us and knew we would be where we are right now, in this place and at this time. Nothing is by chance or by accident. God goes before us and orders our steps. He has never been taken by surprise or caught off guard. He is our constant advocate, faithfully interceding on our behalf. He devotedly works all things together for our good in all circumstances.

It's an amazing thought that, with a request merely whispered from our lips, we can commune one-on-one with the God who spoke the universe into existence. Regardless of our circumstances, He offers peace that surpasses understanding, joy beyond measure, contentment in all things, grace that is more than sufficient, truth that endures to all generations, goodness and mercy that will follow us all the days of our lives, unconditional love that never changes and never fails, and abundant answers for every issue of life.

Since we are all works-in-progress, we can know that nothing we go through is ever wasted or without meaning. I've learned that as we are immersed in the seasons of life, rather than being perplexed, we can come through them enriched, energized, and possessing greater insight.

Anyone can become privy to these dazzling glimpses into God's sovereign design. The key is to pay attention so we don't miss anything. One thing I know for certain: There is always plenty going on.

Some God Stories are conclusive; we can see a beginning and an end. Yet sometimes we see only a few small pieces to a larger puzzle. We can't always know the ending to all of our experiences because sometimes key details remain hidden from our view.

God reveals to us all we need to know, as the details become pertinent to His plan and purpose for us. As we witness certain revelations, these events can be used to encourage us, to let us know we're on the right path, to assure us we have not been forgotten, or simply to remind us that He knows and loves us.

Every second of every day, I am in awe of this Author of my life. I'm constantly inspired by an ever increasing number of events whereby the only way to make sense of what has happened is to acknowledge, once again, many more spectacular examples in a rich and endless reservoir of God Stories.

CANTALOUPE

Because contemporary Christian artist Babbie Mason and I are best friends and have also cowritten so many songs together, we are often asked how we met.

I know that most people expect to hear that we met at a women's retreat ... at a prayer breakfast ... at an all-day sing-a-long ... or on the fortieth day of a forty-day fast at a spiritual warfare conference. I smile each time as I watch their facial expressions while we tell our tale.

IT WAS A HOT SUMMER DAY and I was headed to the corner grocery with one mission in mind—to find the sweetest, coldest, juiciest cantaloupe I could, and to enthusiastically devour it with gusto.

As I stood before a mountainous display of my favorite summer fruit, happily performing my ritual of smelling, thumping, and squeezing, I was interrupted. From over my right shoulder came a deep and sultry alto voice, posing a question:

"How do they feel?"

I turned around to match a face with the voice and told a beautiful, very pregnant woman that they felt great. We began to chat, and as we did, her speaking voice began to sound somewhat familiar. It finally hit me that she had sung at my church several weeks before. But from the third tier of the balcony, she appeared to be only about an inch in height. Face to face and at ground level, she was much taller.

Babbie Mason was her name and we discussed our mutual love for music. I had just written and demoed my first four gospel songs, so I quickly ran to my car and returned with a tape for her to take home. Then, with our cantaloupes in tow, we exchanged phone numbers and went our separate ways.

Several weeks later, and after her baby arrived, Babbie called me. She said she liked my writing, and we decided to get together and try to cowrite something. It went well, and over the next few months we got together often to write. Not only did we enjoy writing together, it seemed like we'd known each other all of our lives.

One day, I received a brochure in the mail advertising the Christian Music Seminar in Estes Park, Colorado. They offered many seminars about the music industry and had great concerts scheduled each night. But the best part of all was that they offered competitions for songwriters, vocalists, instrumentalists, and groups.

Of course, Babbie and I both knew we should go. Our songs were sure to win, and Babbie could also enter the vocal competition. Although we were both financially strapped, we had a few months to save up for our tuition and competition fees. Then we would head to Colorado.

I got an American Express card and charged an airline ticket. Babbie and her husband had just received a new Texaco card, so they decided to drive out. To save on meals, we all brought enough peanut butter to last the week. We shared the rent on a cabin and split all the costs.

When I arrived in Colorado, I found them sitting in their car outside the registration office waiting for me. Babbie looked exhausted. "Kansas is the longest state in the country," she said wearily.

We checked in. They got the bedroom and I got the couch. Our shower, which had three little tiny streams of water dripping from the nozzle, was so small you could only bathe one side of your body at a time.

We went to register for the seminar and learned that we had both made the Top 20 finals for the songwriting competition. Babbie would compete in her vocal competition the next day at 10 A.M.

Meanwhile I went to sit in on the songwriting critiques. They were brutal. The judges would say discouraging, sarcastic things like, "Don't quit your day job." After being chewed up and spit out by the judges, one of the writers was insisting that one evening during his nightly devotionals, God Himself had given him his song. The judge replied, "No, He didn't. God writes better than that."

People were leaving the building in tears. But after hearing some of the other songs for myself, my confidence soared. I just knew we were definitely going to go home with the prize.

Babbie got back from the doctor's office sporting a huge eye patch. Her cornea had been scratched. She later found out she had made the finals in the vocal competition and would have to perform again in a couple of days. I suggested she go for the sympathy vote and sing "Turn Your Eye [instead of Eyes] Upon Jesus."

As we sat anxiously anticipating our song evaluations, our confidence that we were destined to win was growing. Finally, our turn came—my song first, then Babbie's. The judges cut mine to shreds. I was embarrassed and devastated. Babbie's critique was equally as ugly. We vowed never to write songs again.

Babbie did go on to compete in the vocal finals and we went to all the seminars, trying not to let our disappointment show. That night, instead of attending the concert we splurged and went to a movie. Unfortunately, even buttered popcorn and Gummy Bears couldn't ease our disappointment.

Finally, it came time for the awards to be given out. Babbie came in third in the vocal competition. Then the emcee said they were giving an award to the person who had traveled the farthest to attend. I thought, "Well, at least I should get that. I'm sure no one came from any farther than Atlanta to this stupid place!"

The emcee opened his mouth to proclaim the winner. I flexed my legs and was poised, ready to stand and march toward the podium. "Would Kay Bawa Alla from Ghana please stand?" I rolled my eyes and sighed as everyone else burst into wild applause. A short, little, black man made his way down front and collected his huge trophy. I left for lunch where my peanut butter sandwich awaited. By this time, I just wanted to go home.

Back in Atlanta, my friend Paula met me at the airport with some devastating news. While I was away, the president of our choir and his wife, John and Betsy Hudson, had lost her mother and their four-year-old daughter in a drowning accident.

The frustrating events of my own week suddenly seemed unimportant. That night I prayed that I wouldn't have to see John and Betsy at church the next day. I knew of no words that would adequately express my sympathy for the grief they must be feeling after such unimaginable loss.

But as I got out of my car at church the next morning, they pulled up right next to me. We hugged and cried a lot. I still didn't know what to say, except that if God can paint sunsets, put the stars in place, and conquer death forever, I knew He'd find a way to get them through this.

In the weeks to come, I attempted to write a song that could express the compassion I wanted to convey to my friends. Only fragments of the song would come. Then came the tragic news that a sixteen-year-old friend of mine, Laurie Landt, had been abducted from a parking lot. She was later found raped and murdered. My heart felt fractured. The pain was unbearable. This time the words poured onto the page.

Several weeks later, Babbie and I reconvened. Our hurt feelings had healed and we had both resumed writing, incorporating all we had learned at Estes Park into the process. She shared a new song she had just written entitled "All Rise," which had been inspired by the judication experience at Estes Park. The song talked about how one day we will all stand before God and be judged as we give an account of how we spent our lives here on planet earth. I shared the song I had just written, "He'll Find A Way."

Babbie and I continued to write songs, and a year later we returned to Estes Park, where "All Rise" and "He'll Find A Way" both won in the songwriting competition. Babbie also won the Grand Prize in the overall vocal competition. We learned from our experience that the prize comes after the preparation is completed.

Over the years, Babbie and I have become more like sisters than friends. We have vacationed together, had slumber parties during ice storms, and even spent holidays where we wore sweat suits and no bras.

We have written many more songs together, too.

I have often thought that how Babbie and I met was a divine, supernatural encounter over a mound of cantaloupe. Neither of us could have guessed how important that encounter would prove to be or how much a part of each other's lives we would become. But I know that God knew and I'll bet that as He was fashioning the first cantaloupe, He thought of Babbie and me and smiled.

Great is the LORD, and greatly to be praised.

PSALM 48:1

SAM

Sandi Patty's first album was released eighteen years ago. With over ten million albums sold, she has garnered thirty-five Dove Awards, five Grammys, three platinum albums, five gold albums, and has performed before millions of people, including President and Mrs. George Bush. She has authored three books: *Le Voyage*, an allegory on Christian life, and two children's books entitled *Merry Christmas with Love* and *Sam's Rainbow*.

I distinctly remember the day I visited my neighborhood Christian bookstore and heard what seemed to be Sandi's fifty-four octave range soaring to the stratosphere on her rendition of "Amazing Grace." All I could think of was that I should throw my body over anything in the store that was not shatter-proof to try and prevent the inevitable!

What a thrill it was for to meet Sandi face to face at the Christian Artist Music Seminar in 1985. As I recall that day, I remember thinking we had a lot in common. She, too, was charming, extremely witty, a great hugger, and didn't wear glasses!

I've seen Sandi many times over the past fifteen years. Recently I saw her at an event I coproduced at the Georgia Dome. As we greeted each other I thought to myself, "Wow, Sandi's still amazingly talented, charming, witty, and a great hugger. The only thing that's changed is that behind the scenes we now wear glasses because we're both farsighted as bats!" (Time is such a bandit.)

The following story from Sandi is one I specifically asked her to share because I know her number one priority is to be a wife and mother. Every time I hear this story it gives me goose bumps.

❁ ❁ ❁

B ETWEEN THE TWO OF THEM, Sandi Patty and her husband, Don, have seven children. Although seven is certainly more than enough, they occasionally entertained the possibility of celebrating their love for each other by adopting an eighth child.

Don is adopted, so whenever they talked about adding to their family, they often discussed what an awesome experience adoption would be for them. Because of the special relationship Don had with his dad, adopting a boy would be of special significance to him.

If they were to adopt a baby boy, Don and Sandi would definitely name him Sam, after Don's dad.

The "family addition" discussion usually terminated upon hearing the squeaking brakes of the school bus as it dropped off half a dozen members of their current clan. Within the next hour, each of their children would have to be delivered to an extracurricular activity. Ballet, tap, soccer, softball, baseball, choir rehearsal, and piano lessons are just some of the commitments that were highlighted in multi-colored Magic Marker on the already crowded family calendar.

Then reality would set in. An eighth child? Have we lost our minds?

Still, the consideration of adopting another child never went away.

One day, Sandi finally said, "Okay God, if you want something to happen, You're going to have to just drop a baby in our laps!"

After making that statement, Sandi decided to leave the decision to the Lord.

Several months later, Sandi's friend Shari called in a panic. Shari's husband, Wes, handles private adoptions and he had a baby boy available. Something had fallen through with the couple who was supposed to have adopted him. If he weren't adopted within the next twenty-four hours, the baby would be placed in the welfare system. Shari was calling everyone she could think of and asking if they knew of anyone who might be considering adoption.

"You don't know of anyone do you, Sandi?"

Sandi wondered if God was dropping a baby Sam in their laps.

After hanging up the phone, Sandi and Don gathered the family together to talk and pray about the possibility. All of the kids were immediately ready to go and pick up the baby.

Sandi and Don decided that if another family took the baby in the next twenty-four hours, that would be their answer. If no one else came forward, then maybe adopting this little boy was truly God's will for their family. That night they all left it at that and went to sleep.

The next morning, Sandi and Don talked about all of the reasons why they *shouldn't* adopt a baby. They were just recently married. They already had seven children. Yet something inside was telling both of them that this baby was for them. They were just waiting for further confirmation from the Lord.

Sandi knew one thing for certain, she felt totally compelled to go and see the baby. Not to see if he was beautiful or anything like that. She just needed to see him.

Arrangements were made for Sandi, Don, Shari, and Wes to go see the baby. Before they went in the building, Shari insisted that they stop and pray. Everyone clasped hands. Shari shocked everyone as she said, "Okay, listen God, we need a 'smack you in the face burning bush' here. Don't be subtle. We need to know for sure what Your plan is, so give us a sign."

They walked up the stairs where Sandi, Don, and Wes stood in the waiting room. Shari went in to get the baby.

As Shari wheeled the baby into the room, Sandi noticed that

Shari was crying. She couldn't even speak. Sandi assumed that something was wrong. Perhaps another family had already come forward and Shari was crying because she knew that Sandi and Don had become attached to the idea of adopting. She just wasn't sure.

Finally, Shari pointed to the end of the little acrylic bassinet. There was a heart-shaped nametag with rainbows all around it. Although the nurses never name the babies who are to be adopted, for some reason they had named this baby, "SAM."

As they all joined Shari weeping, Sandi began saying, "I can't believe they named him Sam!"

Several of the nurses overheard her and, thinking she was upset about the name, began assuring her that she didn't have to keep that name. It would be perfectly fine to call him anything she wanted to. The nurses didn't realize that the name they chose was all part of God's perfect plan.

The next day, Sandi and Don brought home Samuel Patrick Peslis. His descent is African-American, Native-American, and Caucasian. And now at the age of two, little Sam can also sing in Spanish. Sam is the light of their lives and has brought incredible joy to their home.

❁ ❁ ❁

When the fullness of the time had come, God sent forth His Son, born of a woman, born under the law, to redeem those who were under the law, that we might receive the adoption as sons, and daughters. And because you are sons, and daughters, God has sent forth the Spirit of His Son into your hearts, crying out, "Abba Father!" Therefore you are no longer a slave but a son, or a daughter, and if a son, or a daughter then an heir of God through Christ.

GALATIANS 4:4

GOD'S MERCY
IS NEW EVERY MORNING

Brett Butler played baseball in the major leagues for seventeen years with five different clubs: the Braves, the Indians, the Giants, the Mets, and the Dodgers. He lives in Duluth, Georgia, with his wife, Eveline, and their four children, Abbi, Stefanie, Katie, and Blake. In retirement, Brett and Eveline have started a summer ministry called Winning in Life's Decisions (W.I.L.D.), a program to help teens make the right decisions about life.

Our mutual friend, Chuck Tilley, who produces many of the major music festivals throughout the country, thought Brett's triumph over cancer was a story of faith, trust, and hope for anyone who may be facing a similar battle. I found Brett to be generous with his time, and kind and meticulous in telling me his story.

❋ ❋ ❋

IT WAS THE WINTER OF 1995. Prior to leaving for spring training, Brett Butler scheduled an appointment with his friend and physician, Bob Gadlage, to examine his sore throat. The diagnosis was tonsillitis and the treatment was an antibiotic regimen. The baseball great headed off to south Florida for training.

But after several weeks and three different prescriptions for antibiotics, Brett again contacted Dr. Gadlage. After another examination, Dr. Gadlage told Brett that his throat really didn't look that bad, but eventually, he would probably need to have his tonsils removed. Brett agreed and got another prescription for antibiotics.

About a month into the season, Brett's throat was getting worse. Even though he was playing well, Tommy LaSorda called Brett into his office, telling him that he looked a little tired. He suggested a couple of days off to rest.

Instead, Brett decided to take off five or six weeks. He wanted to get the tonsillectomy out of the way, recuperate, and get back to normal.

Brett and Eveline met Dr. Gadlage at the hospital. Brett was already being sedated when Dr. Gadlage arrived to do his final exam before surgery. As he looked at Brett's throat, Dr. Gadlage stepped back, a little shocked and not exactly sure what he was seeing. When Eveline asked how long the procedure would take, Dr. Gadlage told her 30 to 40 minutes.

Two and a half hours later, Dr. Gadlage came out of surgery and assured Eveline that Brett was all right, but that he had yet to remove his tonsils. He further explained that an oncologist had been called in and would be arriving shortly to assist him. Eveline was more than a little unsettled.

For the surgery to proceed, it was necessary for Brett's jaw to be dislocated. The doctors then removed a plum-sized tonsil, as well as the one that wasn't enlarged.

Following surgery, Dr. Gadlage told Eveline it did not look like cancer, but they would still do a biopsy. He expected the results within a couple of days.

After Brett went home, he quickly realized that even antibiotics and pain pills couldn't relieve the excruciating pain. To swallow, he had to get into a crouched position and grit his teeth. It was agonizing.

A couple of days later, Dr. Gadlage arrived at the Butler home. Brett and Eveline suspected the worst, because they knew if the news had been good, their friend would probably have just telephoned.

Dr. Gadlage came into the house and asked to speak to the two of them in private. They all went into Brett's study where Dr. Gadlage delivered the terrible news.

"Brett, you've got squamous cell cancer."

Immediately upon hearing those words, they noticed that the clear skies outside had suddenly become black. It began to hail. Brett lapsed into a state of semi-shock. He was trying to comprehend what this would mean for himself, his family, his career and his future.

Brett and Eveline called their four children into the room and allowed them to ask the doctor any questions that they had. Because Brett's mom had recently died of brain cancer, the children were already knowledgeable about chemotherapy and radiation. The questions flowed for quite some time.

After the questions subsided, Dr. Gadlage left their home. Simultaneously, as if to acknowledge the departure of the darkness and devastation that had just enveloped their lives, the sun returned again.

Much later, Brett came to understand that even with aggressive treatment, his type of cancer usually returns within a year. For the first week after hearing about the cancer, he was devastated and mad at God: "I went through my checklist, reminding God of how I had lived my life for Him and how I had always tried to follow Him."

But after a time, Brett felt God telling him that if he was willing to accept all the good that God had sent his way, he had to accept the bad, too. Brett understood and began asking God to show His purpose and plan for this situation. Brett needed wisdom and an understanding of how God was going to use this circumstance.

About ten days later, Mark Jones, a man Brett and his wife had sponsored to go to Russia, and Mark's pastor paid Brett and Eveline a visit.

The pastor shared with Brett what God had told him that Brett wasn't just a ball player, but a minister who played ball, that Brett was not going to die, and that God was going to use Brett in a powerful way.

Brett had already begun to sense God's peace; this pastor's words further confirmed that God would undoubtedly work all things together for good.

Brett had to have a second surgery, where they resected the same area and did a total neck dissection, cutting from the bottom of his ear, down his clavicle and across the front to his Adam's apple. They took out fifty lymph nodes. One was malignant. Thirty-two rounds of radiation followed the procedure.

Brett's weight fell from 160 to 142 pounds. The doctors told him that he would never play ball again. Brett, refusing to give up, decided to try alternative medical treatments in Mexico. The treatments were yielding tremendous results, but weren't approved by the FDA. From Mexico, he returned to New Orleans, where his physical fitness expert, Mackie Shilstone, put him on a strict dietetic regimen. He gained 18 pounds in nineteen days.

Four months later, he returned to the big leagues. The response from fifty thousand fans was amazing! It was a tribute to the truth that with God, nothing is impossible. Brett's recovery thoroughly baffled the doctors, who had told him he would never play again.

Five days later, he was hit in the hand while executing a bunt. The impact broke his hand.

Eveline, who had always remained calm and poised during the entire cancer ordeal, was beginning to question God. She didn't understand why He would allow Brett to come through all he had, just to break his hand.

Brett was now the calm one: "I felt God telling me that He was pleased with how I had used this situation to glorify Him. Now it was time to rest. Eveline wanted me to retire, as did our children." Brett, however, wanted to go out in his own way and in God's perfect timing.

In 1997, Brett played the entire season and then retired.

"God had been glorified through it all and He had never given me more than I could handle," he said. "I learned firsthand that God's mercy is new every morning. It is this hope that continues to guide me and my family, assuring us of God's faithfulness every day of our lives."

❀ ❀ ❀

"I know the plans that I have for you," declares the LORD,
"plans to help you prosper and not harm you, plans to give
you a hope and a future."

JEREMIAH 29:11, NIV

THE POWER OF LOVE

Cheryl Landon, daughter of Michael Landon, is an educator, lecturer, and author of the book *I Promised My Dad*. Cheryl tours the country doing her Highway to Success Seminars where she carries on the legacy of love her father left to her. She also co-hosts her own radio show called *The Cheryl Landon Radio Show with Cheryl and Mel*.

When Cheryl received my facsimile requesting an interview, she personally phoned me back. Her call came at 9 A.M. EST, which is only 6 A.M. in Los Angeles. I wasn't out of bed yet, but tried my best to act semi-conscious. Cheryl was excited. I remember thinking that her enthusiasm could probably be harnessed and used to light the entire planet in the event we suffer any type of millennium blackout! We scheduled our interview for after the Christmas holidays. Her story is a wonderful account of how God works even the bleakest circumstances to bring everything together for a greater good.

❁ ❁ ❁

B ECAUSE HER PARENTS WERE DIVORCED, Cheryl's mom worked fulltime to make ends meet. Her earliest childhood memories were feelings of loneliness and not fitting in.

At seven years of age, it all changed when her mom married Michael Landon. Her new dad filled her days with unconditional love, total acceptance, and consistent nurturing. Cheryl Landon's young heart quickly declared Michael as her knight in shining armor.

19

Cheryl blossomed during her college years in Tucson, Arizona, excelling both academically and socially. In her junior year, she was invited to attend a fraternity party, billed as the biggest party of the year.

To help discourage the students from drinking and driving, a bus had been hired to take everyone to the desert where the frat party was being held. When the party ended, the same bus would then bring them back to campus.

Cheryl's sorority sister, Cathy, asked her if she wanted to go to the party with a blind date, along with her and her boyfriend. Cheryl consented. The guys didn't attend the college and were to drive up from Long Beach, California.

The bus was loaded and ready to leave, but their dates had yet to arrive. Cheryl really wanted to board the bus and just leave word for the guys to meet them there, but Cathy insisted they stay and wait for them.

Their dates finally showed up, driving a Volkswagen Beetle. It was a long, two-hour drive from the campus to the desert party, but finally they made it.

The party was loud and high-spirited and the alcohol flowed freely. Before long, many students became inebriated, and soon it was time to go back to campus. Once again, a voice in Cheryl's head was pulling her toward boarding the bus, but Cathy wouldn't hear of it. She insisted that they go back in the car along with their dates. Cheryl didn't want to offend anyone, so she agreed to ride back in the Volkswagen.

There are no streetlights in the middle of the desert and as the bus pulled out, it headed down a dark and desolate highway.

Only a few seconds behind, Cheryl's date started to pull onto the road. He popped the clutch, the car stalled, and everything in the car went dead. At that moment, a Buick driven by a drunk driver going 80 mph raced around the curve. The driver never saw the Volkswagen before it drove directly into them.

The crash sounded like a bomb had exploded. The Volkswagen was airborne for the length of a football field. It flipped over three times in one direction and twice in another, totally demolishing the car.

Cheryl was awake the entire time. She watched Cathy going out, and then coming in the back window, splitting her head wide open. Cathy's boyfriend was decapitated. Cheryl's date was thrown onto the floorboard and then he was flung right onto her. Trapped inside the car, he bled to death as he lay on top of her.

Cheryl sustained numerous traumatic injuries—ruptured organs, a broken neck, and all of her ribs were broken on the left side. Her head was split open from ear to ear. She had sustained massive internal bleeding and her body was totally mangled. Yet, she still remained conscious.

Emergency service vehicles arrived and used the Jaws of Life to take off the door to the Beetle. They pulled Cheryl's date off of her and saw that she was still alive. Totally covered in blood, they couldn't tell who she was or what she looked like, but Cheryl remembers the emergency attendant saying that he thought she might be a pretty girl.

Although only one of her lungs was functioning, Cheryl was afraid and tried fighting the paramedics off with all of her might. The deflated lung had been punctured by one of her ribs, which had also pierced her spleen. But because she was fighting the paramedics off with such tenacity, it kept her good lung breathing for her. She had a tremendous will to live.

Cheryl's mom and dad were notified of the accident by phone. They were in California and with no flights available, her dad had to charter a private plane. Her parents were told the news that Cheryl had yet to learn: Everyone else had been killed in the accident.

Due to a severe concussion, the doctors had to perform several surgical procedures on Cheryl without the use of anesthetics. They were forced to physically restrain her. Finally, when they pushed a tube through her chest into her lungs, the pain was so excruciating that she passed out and fell into a coma.

When her parents arrived at the hospital, the doctors took them into a private area and told them what had been withheld over the phone. Cheryl was dying and they didn't expect her to live through the night. It would take a miracle for her to survive.

Immediately, her dad, Michael, and her mother, Lynn, went into the chapel in the hospital. Michael made what he claimed to be the most important promise of his life. He promised God that if Cheryl survived, he would dedicate all of his future shows and projects to the betterment of all humankind.

Cheryl's parents then went into her room and sat by her bed. Although the nurses insisted that Cheryl couldn't hear him, Michael never lost hope and continually talked to her.

After three days, Cheryl came out of her coma. All of the nurses began to call her a miracle. They were certain God had a special purpose for her life. Michael added that he knew she had been pulled back to life by what he called "the power of love."

Unfortunately, there would be more obstacles to overcome. Cheryl had an insatiable passion for dancing. She was quite accomplished and had won a university dance contest two years in a row. The doctors told Cheryl that she would never be able to dance again. The prognosis was that she would be crippled and in a wheelchair for the rest of her life.

Moreover, Cheryl adored children, and ever since she was sixteen, she had looked forward to the day she would become a mother. She was also given the devastating news that that day would never come.

Cheryl dreamed of becoming a teacher and was now wondering who would ever want to hire her with all of her handicaps. Cheryl sank into a dark depression and sought to find a meaning amidst the ashes.

Meanwhile, her father went on to fulfill his promise to God through his involvement with *Little House on the Prairie* and *Highway to Heaven*. On *Little House on the Prairie*, he developed an episode where Mary went blind. That story line and the episodes to follow were based on some of the similar physical and emotional struggles that Cheryl had faced.

"My family continued to be loving and supportive. After a time, I began studying the Bible. Because of that, my entire life began to change and I made the commitment to turn my life over to Jesus Christ."

Against all odds, Cheryl now manages to do some occasional dancing. God has also blessed her with a beautiful son, James-Michael.

"It is my desire to teach others how to love in today's chaos, because when we love, we bring out the best in each other." The format of her radio program promotes love, harmony, and wholeness, with the goals to promote positive living and to teach her listeners to replace fear with wisdom and faith.

Like her dad, Cheryl believes that "God is love and that the power of love is the strongest force in the universe. I am living proof that love can cast out fear, overcome difficulty and bring about miraculous changes." That is the true power of love.

❀ ❀ ❀

For God has not given us a spirit of fear, but of power and of love and of a sound mind.

2 TIMOTHY 1:7

REMEMBER THE SABBATH
DAY TO KEEP IT HOLY

Michael Medved is a nationally known and highly respected author, film critic, and host of a nationally syndicated radio show. Over the years, I've read print reviews and have watched Michael's commentary on his PBS television show *Sneak Preview*.

I once had the opportunity to hear Michael in person at a banquet for the Christian Film and Television Commission and found what he had to say to be all-inspiring. Having the opportunity to interview him was truly an honor.

Here is his story.

❀ ❀ ❀

I N THE POST-PROPHETIC PERIOD of Jewish tradition, it is be lieved that the voice of God is heard through the law and through one's pattern of obligations and behavior.

Michael Medved had been observing the Sabbath, as well as all Jewish holidays, for over twenty-five years. With this decision comes a total commitment to the things of God from sundown Friday night till sundown Saturday night.

In the Jewish tradition, Michael honors God by withdrawing from active involvement in the business world for twenty-four hours. Although the Sabbath is an active day, there is no exchange of money, no television, radio, or movies, and no driving.

Instead, concentration is centered around family, worship, and enjoying the world the way God created it to be, rather than fulfilling the desire for material success, prominence, and passion to change the world.

In 1984, Michael released a book that he co-wrote with his brother, titled *Hollywood Hall of Shame*. It was very well received and its content examined some of the biggest financial disasters in Hollywood history.

When the book came out, Michael was offered the opportunity to promote *Hollywood Hall of Shame* as a guest on *The Tonight Show*. It was the dream of a lifetime.

Joan Rivers was guest hosting the show and she and Michael had worked together before. She was excited about his book and invited him to come and talk about it on the show. Needless to say, he was thrilled and as excited as any young author would be.

The Tonight Show called to give Michael the date for his appearance—the first night of Passover. Michael explained that he really wanted to be on the show but that he absolutely couldn't be on during the Passover celebration. He further conveyed some of the restrictions during the Jewish holidays.

The producer told him that he really shouldn't worry about it because the religious people Michael was concerned about wouldn't be watching the show that night anyway.

"Yes, but the idea isn't that the other people won't see it. The point is that God will be watching and I just can't do it," Michael replied.

The producers conceded and elected to respect Michael's convictions. The conversation ended with a promise to schedule an alternative date.

A couple of hours later, the producers called back saying that Joan Rivers really wanted him to do the show. They offered Michael a second date six days later.

The biblical injunction of Passover is that the first two days be totally devoted to the Lord and then no work during the last days. The alternative date for *The Tonight Show* fell during the last days of the holiday.

Michael told the producers, "You aren't going to believe it, but you've just hit another one of those days during the holiday when I can't work."

In only a few moments, the producer phoned back and told Michael that he'd surveyed the Jewish constituents in his office and found that no one else even practiced this holiday.

Michael got out the biblical citation and read it to him.

The producer responded by telling Michael that he was beginning to think Michael didn't really want to do the show. Michael assured him that was not the case and that he was very eager to do the show. He just couldn't violate the patterns of his religious observance.

As they ended the conversation, Michael thought for certain that he'd not be extended another invitation. He even experienced a few days of feeling martyred, as though his sacrifice might have been beyond the call of reasonable devotion.

Being on *The Tonight Show* would be a positive career step and one that anyone seeking mass exposure dreamed of. Michael had twice turned down that chance due to religious consciousness. He also had the feeling that no one in the industry understood his reasoning and that soon he would become a laughingstock because of his unbending rigor.

Much to his amazement, however, and within only a couple of days, *The Tonight Show* producer called back and cheerfully offered Michael a third date for his appearance. This time the date worked.

Michael did the show. Joan Rivers was extremely nice to him and the experience was very positive.

The next morning, Michael got a call from Chicago from one of the producers of the PBS show *Sneak Preview*. The producer had seen his appearance on *The Tonight Show*, thought Michael to be articulate and funny, and was interested in flying him to Chicago to talk with him about becoming involved with their program.

Michael flew to Chicago. During the meeting with the producer of *Sneak Preview*, the producer stressed to Michael that he rarely watched late-night television and hadn't seen *The Tonight Show* in three years. He further explained that he had been over at his girlfriend's house "channel surfing" and had just happened to catch Michael's interview. Again and again he stressed how unlikely it had been that he had even seen Michael's interview!

As a result of *The Tonight Show* interview, Michael was hired as the host of *Sneak Preview*. He worked for the next twelve years reviewing films from a pro-family perspective.

"If I had appeared on *The Tonight Show* the first time I was invited, the producer of *Sneak Preview* would never have seen my interview. Therefore, the chances are good that I would never have been hired for the job I had for twelve of the nineteen years that *Sneak Preview* was on the air. I honored God by keeping my commitment to Him. And by being the good, loving, and caring God that He always is, God honored me."

"Even when we think we are making a sacrifice, if it is in an effort to follow God and if it is done in His name and out of devotion to Him, the chances are good we'll be rewarded for it, even in this life!"

❀ ❀ ❀

Remember the Sabbath day by keeping it holy. Six days you shall labor and do all your work, but the seventh day is the Sabbath to the LORD your God. In it you shall not do any work ... for in six days the LORD made the heavens and the earth, the sea, and all that is in them, but he rested on the seventh day. Therefore the LORD blessed the Sabbath day and made it holy.

EXODUS 20:8-11, NIV

27

In All Things Give Thanks

I T WAS A COLD JANUARY DAY when Babbie and I sat on an
Atlanta Delta flight bound for Nashville. This was an excit-
ing day because it was our first trip to "Music City" after winning the songwriting competition at Estes Park. We were headed
there to demo seven of our newly written songs, after which we
could pitch them to various artists and producers, in hopes of
getting them recorded.

For what seemed like forever, we waited for the plane to take
off. The flight attendants began offering free beverages to everyone. Babbie was reading a book. I was doing my homework for
a class called Continuing Witness Training, where I was learning
how to share my faith in a concise and effective manner.

After about forty-five minutes of waiting, we decided to stand
up and stretch our legs. As we did, we overheard a young woman
having a conversation with a male passenger. He was asking what
she did for a living. She told him she was Miss Nashville and
that, in addition to the duties that went along with the title, she
traveled with her family doing concerts on weekends. We decided to jump into the conversation.

"What kind of music?" we asked her.

"Gospel," she said with a smile.

We told her why we were going to Nashville. Spontaneously,
and as a joke, we formed an a cappella trio and, unsolicited,
began to belt out the chorus of "I'll Fly Away."

At the conclusion of our song, a voice over the PA informed

us that our plane could not be repaired. They were moving us to a room inside the terminal where everyone would continue to receive free drinks while they located a new plane for us.

As the 230 passengers filed into the room awaiting us, Babbie, Miss Nashville, and I continued to sing familiar hymns. By now, many of the passengers were getting tipsy, while others were just downright loaded. We may have been the only three sober passengers left.

After about thirty minutes, we decided to bring an end to our musical interlude by singing "Amazing Grace." As we did, an "amazing" thing happened—passengers began putting down their drinks and gathering around us. Many sang along. Some wept. Others just bowed their heads in silence.

At the conclusion of our impulsive mini-concert, we had the opportunity to talk with several people about our faith in God and what knowing Him means to us. I whipped out the notes from a witness training class and began going down the checklist of questions to ask. Some people told us how they had slipped away from their relationship with the Lord and we had the chance to encourage them. It was an incredible experience.

At that moment, our plane became ready and soon we were airborne.

Our publisher, Adel Mizenheimer, and our host, Cindy Wilt, were waiting for us at the airport in Nashville. We stepped off the plane and they embraced us.

"You poor babies," they said. "You must be exhausted."

Exhausted? Not us! We were invigorated. We'd just had a revival at the airport.

The next morning, Babbie and I were sipping Cindy's freshly brewed vanilla bean coffee and reading the Bible. A bit nervous at what was in front of us, we asked God to encourage us by giving us a passage that would apply to our upcoming day. Babbie decided to "drop and flop." (You hold your Bible outward, let it drop and flop open, and then you point. Wherever your finger lands, that's what you read. A deeply spiritual approach, we have always felt!)

Babbie's finger was pointing to Psalm 31:21: *Blessed be the* LORD, *for He has shown me His marvelous kindness in a strong city!*

Okay, we were ready to conquer the world!

We made our demos and came home on Sunday. The pitching process began on Monday, and by Thursday all of our songs had been spoken for, some of them more than once! We had been told that the average working songwriter might get two songs published a year, but by the end of that year, we had over thirty songs recorded between the two of us.

Several years later, I was a couple of days away from making one of my trips to Los Angeles. I was scheduled to stay there for a week, but only two of the twenty or so people I wanted to see had returned my calls to schedule an appointment. A bit discouraged, I decided to forget everything for a couple of hours and go to the mall for a Saturday afternoon movie.

Getting there was a challenge because we were having heavy thunderstorms. I ran from my car into the mall where, totally soaked, I ran into Babbie. She was buying a blouse and was en route to the airport headed to "Somewhere, USA" to perform a concert.

I told her what I was doing there and why, and she reminded me of the psalm that had encouraged us several years ago.

We parted ways and I went to my movie.

After the movie, I went to my car to discover that the driver's side window had been bashed in. The front seat was rain-soaked and glass was everywhere. Because I never carry a purse, someone who was checking out the parking lot probably assumed my wallet had been left under the seat.

After filing a police report, I removed as much of the glass as I could and sat down on the drenched seat to make my way home. My backside was soaked and, as I drove, the hard rain continued to blow onto my face and upper body. Needless to say, this was not one of my favorite days.

When I got home, I got out the Yellow Pages to try and figure out where I should go to have my window repaired. I first looked

30

under "window" and didn't see anything. Then I looked under "glass" and couldn't believe what was staring back at me. There was a full-page ad for glass repair. In bold black print at the bottom of the page, was the verse: *Blessed be the* LORD, *for He has shown me His marvelous kindness in a strong city!* In a glass repair advertisement!

I tracked Babbie down and told her to turn to page 1023 of her Yellow Pages to see if the ad was in her book, too. (I thought it would be just like God to have it only in mine!) When I finally found her, Babbie's response was priceless.

"Wow," she exclaimed, "this is like opening up your closet and seeing a scripture like John 3:16 stitched to your blouse."

I had my car repaired and left for Los Angeles. When I got to my hotel and checked in, I told the Lord I was there on His behalf. And by the time I returned to the hotel, everyone I wanted to see had called me back. I was able to meet with all of them.

Holding on to our dreams and standing on our faith can be challenging when we can't see past our immediate circumstances.

Countless times, I've been blessed with a favorable outcome to the goals I've pursued. Equally as often, success has eluded me. It is through all of these experiences that I've gained knowledge and wisdom. Understanding this, I am convinced that the times of difficulty are gifts to us, as are the victories.

God is always with us, working everything together for His purpose and for our good. And for that, we can truly give thanks in all things.

❁ ❁ ❁

Do not be afraid or dismayed ... for the battle is not yours but God's.

2 CHRONICLES 20:15

CHOOSE JOY!

Probably best known for playing Laura Holt in her long-running television series *Remington Steele*, costarring Pierce Brosnan, Stephanie Zimbalist is one of the most loved and widely sought-after actresses in Hollywood. With a long string of *Movie of the Week* roles and feature films to her credit, she's also been recognized as a successful stage actress and continues to tread the boards. She recently returned to television with a guest appearance on the award-winning series *Touched by an Angel*. Currently, she's just completed a leading role in an independent film titled *The Prophet's Game*, with Dennis Hopper.

On the day of our phone interview, I was particularly taken by Stephanie's warmth and approachability, although I found myself distracted a couple of times with the thought that I was speaking with someone who had actually kissed James Bond.

A few hours following our interview that day, Stephanie phoned back and read me some additional information from her journal to give me some further insight into her story. Needless to say, I was overwhelmed by her generosity of time, sincerity, and concern that I had all I needed to write her story. Her kind-heartedness was truly refreshing.

❀ ❀ ❀

R EARED IN A FAMILY with practically every species in the animal kingdom Stephanie Zimbalist comes by her immense
love for animals naturally. Flamingos, ocelots, Brazilian
trumpters, peacocks, deer, dogs, and horses alike were all welcomed at the Zimbalist house.

In 1987, just before Christmas, Stephanie's mother was driving along the access road to a freeway when she spotted a tiny,
soiled, white, fluffy puppy scampering along beside her. Certain
that the tiny dog was lost and terrified, she followed it until it
collapsed in a yard.

As Mrs. Zimbalist got a closer look, she noticed that the pup
was gnarled, matted, and appeared to be in pretty bad condition.
She scooped it up, put it in the car, and off they went to the vet.

She was about three months old and a combination of Malt-
ese, Westie, Cockapoo, and Wheaten Terrier. Her ears had never
been trimmed and the little wisps of hair protruding from them
looked remarkably like angel's wings. She had a soulful tender-
ness in her eyes that hinted of an uncanny ability to read the
human spirit like an open book. After the vet had cleaned her
up, Mrs. Zimbalist took the little orphan home and introduced
her to the other eight dogs—her new family!

Full of energy and grateful to be where she was loved, the
little dog consistently greeted everyone by jumping up and down,
dipping, and twirling about until she would nearly drop from
exhaustion. Stephanie dubbed her the "circus dog."

Sometime later, while in New York performing in *The Baby
Dance*, Stephanie found herself stopping every dog on the street
to talk, pet, or play. She knew it was time to have another dog of
her own.

Upon returning to Los Angeles, Mrs. Zimbalist suggested
Stephanie take Meggie. Since there were nine dogs at the Zimbalist
house, Stephanie asked, "Which one's Meggie?"

"The one you call the circus dog," her mother said.

"Oh, that's a sweet dog," Stephanie replied. "She'll be perfect." And off they went to Stephanie's house.

Within a very short time, Stephanie renamed the circus dog Dippy. She decided it was the only name that truly suited her!

Dippy and Stephanie became complete, inseparable companions.

Two weeks later, Stephanie was hired to do an ABC movie in Vancouver, and Dippy took her first airplane ride. In fact, the adorable terrier accompanied her "mom" on all of her subsequent film shoots. Stephanie called Dippy her "ambassador of good will."

Whenever Dippy trotted into a room, smiles broke out and arms unfolded and opened up. She'd roll over with her paws extended and her belly in full view, beckoning a scratch from any who dared. Even the hardest heart would melt!

In 1996, Stephanie was going away for the summer to play the part of Sylvia in A.R.Gurney's enchanting play, *Sylvia*. The play is about a very savvy New York couple whose lives are turned upside down by Sylvia, a homeless stray dog.

On June 12 Stephanie met with her contractor to discuss some post-earthquake work that needed to be done while she and Dippy were away. They sat outside in Stephanie's gazebo having lunch as they went over the details of the repairs.

"Dippy, who was sitting on the man's lap, suddenly got up on the table and walked over to me. She looked intently into my eyes with such a penetrating look of deep love that it actually startled me."

" My gaze was suddenly drawn to my right where my eyes fell upon a patch of bare ground behind the gazebo. I felt a distinct inexplicable sadness and thought to myself that I needed to plant something there to offset the bare ground and dead fern."

"At 5:30 A.M. the next morning, the shrill cacophony of at least fifty crows in my front yard awakened me. I opened my front door and, not wanting to wake the neighbors, clapped my hands a few times at the crows, to no avail. They only flew to the next tree."

Stephanie called to Dippy: "C'mon, Dip!"

But no Dippy. Assuming she was back inside, Stephanie closed the door.

Dippy had always slept on her mistress's bathrobe at the foot of her bed, but when Stephanie returned to her bedroom, Dippy wasn't there.

"I went back outside and called to Dippy once more, but still no response. At this point my heart began to pound as terror rose."

"I looked at the laundry door, saw the open doggie door, and started to panic. Stepping out back and calling for Dippy, I was stunned to see a huge coyote pacing the back fence. My heart fell to my feet as I let out a howl I never knew a human being could be capable of."

"I raced up the hill and there behind the gazebo on the very spot of barren ground that had eerily summoned me the day before, Dippy lay lifeless, her back totally ripped open. As I screamed in disbelief, I saw the last little movement of Dippy's muzzle, as if saying goodbye."

Gently, she lifted Dippy up, wrapped her in a towel, and rushed her to a twenty-four-hour animal hospital.

"In total shock, I raced through several red lights and I prayed. Sobbing and grief-stricken as I drove, the words caught in my throat, 'Dip, if you are meant to stay here with me, hold on. But if you must go, may you fly swiftly and joyously to your Maker.'

"Glancing back I saw her precious dog's paw jostled by the car's motion, waving good-bye."

As desperately as Stephanie had hoped and prayed for a different outcome, it would not be. Praying on the floor of the vet's waiting room didn't help. Dip had died.

"In complete shock and wrenching grief, three weeks after Dippy's passing I found myself in New York fulfilling my previous commitment and following Dippy's heavenly directive by rehearsing for the role as the dog in *Sylvia*."

At the end of the play, Sylvia has passed on and her owner, Greg, comes to the edge of the stage and says to the audience, "I think I have a picture of Sylvia. Let me show you." He then reaches into his back pocket just as an enormous photograph of a dog descends into view. (This is the first time the audience gets to see a real dog, because throughout the play Stephanie has been on her hands and knees playing the role of the dog.)

"This performance was my homage to Dip, guided by Dip. I had requested that the photograph revealed to the audience be one of Dippy. For one last time Dippy and I were together. It was the hardest thing I had ever done and the best."

The tour was extremely successful and Stephanie went on to do a long run of the Los Angeles premiere of the play.

"Months passed, but the loss of my angel dog tore at my heart. I prayed, I wrote, I talked to my Maker, to *our* Maker. But whenever I dreamed of Dippy or closed my eyes to conjure up her image, all that came to me was that grizzly final picture in the backyard."

In her journal, six months after Dippy died, is this entry:

"Last week sometime, or maybe two weeks ago, I got a wrenching, vivid re-visitation of Dippy's last moments. I burst into sobs . . . tears, got down on my knees by my bed, head in hands, and cried, 'Please, please! Give me another picture of your life!!

And a voice, a thought, clear as a bell, came back to me gently, 'Give me another picture of your *life.'*

I struggle to see past Dippy's gruesome, anguishing, tortured, agonizing tunnel from this world. I struggle to see her in the Other World . . . the Other Side . . . the New World . . . Heaven. And she came to me and her Master came to me with these words, 'Give me *another picture of* your *life! That is to say,* I *am in pain here, my beloved mistress, as I look down and know that you are in pain, you are grief-stricken, you are lost. If you want to help me with my pain, if you want to see me in joy where I am now, then give me a new picture of* your *life. Make a new life for yourself. Make a new beginning. Choose joy!'*"

Saying good bye is never easy. When we are wounded and hurting from such a loss, it is God's deepest priority to tenderly and compassionately heal us. Isn't it amazing how He so gently embraced Stephanie's brokeness with such a perfectly individualized response, designed specifically to comfort her?

The way in which Stephanie's prayer was answered was profound and deeply personal. It came to her in a way that she could understand, a healing arrow into her heart.

"It was a gift to me from Dippy, my Cloud of Heaven, and from her Master. It was a gift for which I've been forever grateful."

God has given us an abundance of wonderful gifts . . . love, compassion, laughter, tears . . . and still, even in the midst of great adversity, He has gifted us with the ability to choose joy!

❀ ❀ ❀

A bruised reed He will not break, and a smoking flax He will not quench. . . .

ISAIAH 42:3

A Place Called Surrender

Premiere percussionist, and the protégée of The Artist Formerly Known As Prince, Sheila E comes by her rhythmic ability honestly. The "E" is short for Escovedo, as in legendary percussionist Pete Escovedo, Sheila's dad. Pete Escovedo secured his place in the music business as the drummer for Santana. Sheila has played backup music for internationally known artists such as Diana Ross, Herbie Hancock, Lionel Richie, Marvin Gaye, George Duke, Placido Domingo, Babyface, Natalie Cole, Patti LaBelle, and Gloria Estefan. In addition to recording numerous solo albums, she is one of the most highly sought-after studio percussionists in the world.

I interviewed Sheila E between recording sessions from her studio in Los Angeles. Her love for God came through loud and clear. The last thing she said to me at the completion of our interview was that if I ever had any other projects I needed her for, the answer was yes before I called. Her pliability and willingness to be used of God without question blew me away.

In 1990, Sheila E was working on her fourth solo recording project for Warner Brothers. Being somewhat of a workaholic and having just come off the road with Prince, her body was extremely exhausted—a fact that had yet to make its way to her brain. Totally submerged in her project, Sheila E kept late hours, wasn't eating properly, and got no exercise, outside of when she performed. A few of her friends had even mentioned to her that she wasn't looking well. But loving music and having such a passion for her work, she ignored her friends, as well as some of the obvious hints her body was trying to give her as she pressed toward completing her project.

Unexpectedly and without warning, her lung collapsed. After the doctor completed her examination and assessed the problem, she asked these two questions: "Am I going to die?" and "If I'm not going to die, can you fix it?"

The doctors told her that her lung could be repaired. But Sheila E was sensing a pinnacle of devastation she'd never known before. She was accustomed to being in control and always able to fix things on her own. A collapsed lung was a new frontier.

As soon as she was admitted to the hospital, the surgeons anesthetized her, made their incision, performed a procedure to aspirate the fluid from her lung, re-inflated it, and closed her back up.

Her surgeons prescribed heavy-duty pain medication that she elected not to take. Instead, Sheila E spent a lot of time praying and reading the Bible. She told God that she knew she had been working too hard and needed to learn to do things in moderation. She promised to do better.

After spending a week in the hospital and finally having her stitches removed, she decided to go home to Minneapolis. While there, she could continue healing and visit with her godchildren as well.

During her stay in Minneapolis, Sheila E felt she was regaining some of her strength, but continued to struggle emotionally. There was one cold, hard fact that kept reeling through her mind—she had no control over what was happening to her.

One morning she was bent over in a squat position, playing out in the backyard with her godchildren. As she turned away from them to cough, she threw her back out. In fact, her back was so severely injured that while walking later that evening, her legs folded beneath her and she fell to the floor. She was left with no feeling in her legs.

Her body had shut down. For the next two weeks, her legs remained numb and she had to be carried everywhere. This was the first time in years that she had to pull away from her work, forced to rest and be perfectly still.

The doctor insisted that this time she had to take her medication. Feeling that she had no choice, she complied. Instead of beginning to feel better, however, she started feeling worse.

She would call and give him updates on how badly she felt. He assumed her doldrums were just part of a slow healing process. What neither of them had yet to realize was that the medication for her lung was actually making her sicker.

Her body weight dropped down to eighty-five pounds. Her cousin was force-feeding her because it took all of her strength just to breathe. Sheila E became convinced that she really might be dying.

So she got her Bible and wouldn't let go of it. Even in her weakened state, she read it all day every day and prayed without ceasing. She called out to God to intervene and supernaturally heal her.

Somewhat in desperation, Sheila E finally decided to ask God exactly what He wanted her to do. What she believed He whispered in her ear was clear and simple: He wanted her to completely *surrender* her life to Him.

She began to ponder the idea.

Back in 1978, Sheila E had made somewhat of a commitment to the Lord without understanding what she was supposed to do with such a commitment. It was almost like the politically correct thing to do—to be born again. But it was a decision she had made without further knowledge of what it really meant to be a follower of Christ. The concept of surrendering her life to Jesus and letting Him live His life through her hadn't quite sunk in.

For a month she lay on her back, helpless to do anything but chat with God, listen to Him, and read His Word. The time of forced rest became one of enlightenment, and as her eyes were opened the same prompting came to her again and again. *Surrender. Relinquish control. Give it up. Over and out.*

Surrender was the bottom line—and so surrender she did.

The day finally came when Sheila E felt she might be strong enough to get out of bed and go outside for a little while. She was still slightly apprehensive because she was fearful that being outside might make her sick again.

Then, that still small voice inside reminded her: *In your weakness I am strong.* She quickly dispelled the fear and chose to trust, not in her own ability, but in the One whose strength is made perfect in her weakness.

She proceeded toward the front door. Slowly and cautiously, she made her way outside. As she smelled the fresh air, she began to cry. She breathed in deeply, filling her lungs to capacity. She noticed an array of beautiful multicolored flowers in bloom. Certain that the scent would be magnificent, she leaned down to draw it in.

She moved slowly toward a tree and pressed her back against its trunk. Her body was warmed by the radiant sunshine and with hands uplifted and her face tilted toward heaven, her eyes drank in the perfectly blue sky.

Through tears she began thanking God for everything—for the joy of walking on the grass as it tickled her feet, for the exquisite beauty surrounding her, and mostly for the ability to notice.

But the most amazing revelation of all was that this panoramic view had been there all along and could be viewed at will for free.

Sheila E's heart is still overflowing with gratitude. Not a day goes by that she doesn't thank God for all that belongs to her because she belongs to Him. She believes He gives her mercy that is new every morning, grace that is more than sufficient, goodness that will follow her all the days of her life, peace that passes understanding, limitless unconditional love, compassion that never fails, immeasurable unspeakable joy, and the beauty and wonder of His creation.

DONNA I. DOUGLAS

❀ ❀ ❀

"All to Jesus I surrender, Lord I give myself to Thee;
Fill me with Thy love and power, Let Thy blessings fall
  on me.
I surrender all, I surrender all.
All to Thee my blessed Savior, I surrender all."

(FROM THE HYMN, "I SURRENDER ALL,"
WRITTEN BY JUDSON W. VAN DEVENTER
AND WINFIELD S. WEEDON)

If God Be for Us

Dennis Tinerino is a former Mr. America, Mr. Natural Universe, and a four-time Mr. Universe. He now describes his life's work as one who "travels the world as a minister of the gospel of Jesus Christ."

Dennis is doing a lot of work in the inner cities. He believes that God and only God can turn things around. He has witnessed entire gangs lay down their weapons and weep at the altar, repent of their wrongdoings, and embrace life with fresh attitudes, and embark on new beginnings.

With titles such as Mr. America and Mr. Universe, Dennis Tinerino should have had a bright future ahead of him. Instead, he ended up on the wrong side of the law and spent some time in prison. But what Satan meant for evil, God meant for good, and it was there that he accepted Jesus as his Savior. Since then, he's traveled all over the world spreading the good news of Christ, with a focus on the inner city.

ONE AFTERNOON, DENNIS AND WENDELL TYLER, a running back for the San Francisco '49ers, were having lunch in Palmdale, California. As an outreach to the inner city, a number of other athletes, including Dennis and Wendell, were speaking at a crusade that was being held later that evening. As they talked, Dennis began to feel that he should go home to Northridge and get his wife, Anita, and their children. He wanted them to join him as he spoke at the crusade.

Dennis arrived at home, loaded up everyone in the van, and with Anita at the wheel, they headed back toward the crusade.

It was February and a torrential rainstorm flooded the California highway. As Dennis began to pray about the crusade that evening, the Lord brought a scripture to mind: "Since the days of John the Baptist there has been violence in the heavens, but the violence is taken by force." (Matthew 11:12)

Dennis then told Anita that he sensed the need to pray. He knew that God wanted to do a great work at the crusade that evening and that many lives would be changed as a result of it. He felt people were going to be saved, healed, delivered, and set free, but that Satan wanted to try to stop the works the Lord would accomplish. Anita said she sensed the same thing and they both began to call on God.

Sheets of rain were pouring down and they could hardly see in front of their van. Cars were weaving from lane to lane all around them, and Anita wasn't sure what to do. Dennis grabbed the steering wheel and began to pray aloud: "Satan, I bind you in the name of Jesus!"

Dennis hit the center divider and, as he was bounced from the left side of the car back to the right side, he broke the armrest with his ribs. Anita was flung from the driver's seat over on top of Dennis and lost consciousness.

Dennis continued to pray and praise God as loudly as he could. As he did, he could hear crashing sounds coming from everywhere. It sounded like steel crunching against steel, while torpedoes were going off.

After the van again hit the center divider, it did a 180-degree turn, went onto the right side of the off-ramp, and flipped upside down. When it had completely stopped, the van was turned over on its side and most of the windows were broken. Anita had now been thrown back over into the driver's seat, but they had missed every other car.

The scent of a rose permeated the van, which Dennis recognized as the Rose of Sharon. He had the *peace that passes all understanding* (Philippians 4:7) and kept clinging to II Timothy 1:7, *For God has not given me a spirit of fear but of power, and of love and of a sound mind.*

Dennis heard a knock on the windshield. He looked up, but no one was there. Then he heard a voice saying, *With the peace God gives you, all is well. The enemy is defeated over your life and there is a hedge of Divine protection around you. You are dwelling in the secret place of the Most High and abiding under the shadow of the Almighty.* (Psalm 91:1)

Dennis saw a man looking into the car. The man told Dennis that he had seen the accident and had come to help him.

By this time, the van had filled up with about three feet of water. Dennis turned to look in the backseat and saw that his two-month-old son, DJ, was out of his carseat and face down in the water. There was blood all over him and the seat. As Dennis reached down to pick him up, DJ looked up and smiled at him. The man who had stopped to help had put his coat around the baby.

Next, Dennis looked at his daughter, Tara, who was semiconscious. She looked at Dennis and in a soft, tender voice she said, " I'm okay, Daddy."

Dennis then looked over at Anita, who had also been unconscious. She said she was slightly dizzy, but that she was okay.

In the very back of the van was his other daughter, Marisa. Her body was twisted. Dennis quickly crawled out of the side of the van and made his way to the back of the vehicle to open it up. By this time, there were cars all around and people trying to help.

As Dennis opened up the backseat, he saw that Marisa's head was wedged underneath the seat. A lady came running toward the van and when she saw Marisa, she cried, "Oh no! That poor little girl is dead!"

Undaunted, Dennis began to speak life over her. "Satan, she is not dead. She is alive and will live to declare the works of God!"

As he pulled her out from underneath the seat, he noticed blood coming from her right ear and she had no pulse. Dennis continued, "She will live and not die!"

With that, Marisa opened her eyes and starting breathing. "Daddy, Satan tried to kill us, but the Lord sent the angels. I saw ten-thousand angels. They came from everywhere and said that everything's going to be okay because God is with us."

As Dennis got everyone out of the van, a man approached him and said, "I can't believe this."

The man, who had been driving behind Dennis, told him, "You're the best driver I've ever seen!"

"What do you mean?" asked Dennis.

"When you began to hydroplane, you missed every car, hit the center divider, and still missed every car. You drove this van like you were a stunt man. It looked like it was choreographed."

Dennis exclaimed, "I didn't drive this van! Hallelujah! The Lord drove that van! Praise God!"

The ambulance came and took everyone to the hospital. Everyone checked out just fine, so Dennis decided to go on to the crusade and tell everyone how God had spared and protected his family.

As Dennis stood before the crowds that evening, he told of God's mercy and goodness. Five people were delivered from strongholds in their lives and over one hundred people accepted Christ as their Savior.

The next morning, the entire Tinerino family attended their church and testified what God had done for them.

❁ ❁ ❁

If God be for us, who can be against us?

ROMANS 8:31, KJV

THE DESIRES
OF YOUR HEART

Jeff Kemp was a quarterback for eleven seasons in the NFL with
the Los Angeles Rams, San Francisco '49ers, Seattle Seahawks,
and Philadelphia Eagles. He now serves on the Executive Com-
mittee of Pro Athletes Outreach, which trains athletes to be
responsible role models. Jeff's father, Jack, is a former U.S. Con-
gressman and former Secretary of the Department of Housing
and Urban Development. In 1996, his father was the Republi-
can vice-presidential candidate on the Dole/Kemp ticket. Jeff is
the Executive Director for the Washington Family Council, a
nonprofit research, education, and communications organization that's dedicated to strengthening family relationships, pro-
moting responsible citizenship, and improving public policy in
Washington State.

When I called my friend Jennifer Kemp Andrews and asked
for any suggestions she might have for people I could interview,
three words immediately fired from her lips: "My brother, Jeff!"

I interviewed Jeff on a Friday evening by car phone as he made
his way home from work. And although call-waiting beeped in
often, he politely and apologetically interrupted our interview
only once to take a call from his wife. That spoke volumes to me.
He made me feel important. I really appreciated being given the
sense that what I needed from him was a priority. Jeff's story
reveals that Jeff is a man who seeks after and follows God.

❋ ❋ ❋

Prior to graduating from Dartmouth in 1981, Jeff Kemp realized that something was missing in his life. Even with all his success, including the chance to play professional football for the Los Angeles Rams, there was still something that kept bothering him deep down. He finally concluded that he was missing the joy that comes with an intimate relationship with Christ. God was just an extra piece in his life.

Jeff was raised in a Christian home. He had made a commitment to Christ at an early age, but knew that he had not adhered to that plan during his college years.

During graduate week his mind was flooded with questions. With all the great things he had going on in his life, why did he feel empty, selfish, and insecure? Why was he a follower when his parents had raised him to be a leader?

Maybe he was compromising too many areas of his life. He worried about whether he would make the team with the Rams, and then he worried about being cut from the team. He worried about having a big ego and living without Christ if he did make it to pro football. He knew he needed a change. Christ's purpose for his life needed to be his purpose, as well.

That summer, his transition to California was a good one. He met a lot of the Christian players on the team and they became his new set of friends. Through their Bible studies, they began to disciple him. It became a year of trying to do things God's way.

The month prior to training camp, Jeff stayed with relatives in Laguna Beach, where he stayed focused on football. There wasn't much time for a social life, so he became lonely. He worked out all day and at the end of each day, he went body surfing. Then, a couple of weeks into training camp, he prayed to the Lord about his loneliness and his desire to meet a godly woman.

He continued to work hard and was only off one night a week.

But he knew that God was in control, and in His time would answer that prayer.

A newspaper article was written about Jeff in the local paper in Fullerton, the hub for the Rams boot camp. In the article it said that twenty-five years earlier, his father, Jack, had been a long shot for the same position. Jeff was the fifth of five quarterbacks and they were only keeping three. In the closing comment of the article, the reporter asked Jeff if he was concerned about this and he replied, "No, I'm leaving it in God's hands."

The mother of a USC senior-to-be named Stacy Parker saw the article. Thinking that Jeff sounded like a nice young man, she placed it in front of her daughter's nose and suggested she read it. Stacy politely declined to read the piece. Although she was sure it was a nice article, like Jeff, she had recently come to a similar conclusion about the importance of knowing and following God. She had always had boyfriends in the past, but at this point in time, she was more concerned with developing her relationship with the Lord.

A week or so later, however, Stacy pulled out the article again. She read it and was impressed that Jeff had made a public comment about his faith in God. She worked at the athletic department at USC and asked someone in the office how to get a letter to a Rams player. She secured the address and wrote Jeff a note to encourage him and to tell him that she would be praying for him.

Jeff wrote her back on a piece of crooked notebook paper. At the end of the note, he asked her to excuse him for the stationery, but that that was the best a rookie could do.

Both having pure motives, neither thought anything further about the exchange.

A few weeks later, Stacy was at a church party where one of the people said he knew Jeff and several of the other Rams players from attending a Bible study with them. A group outing had been planned and the friend asked Stacy if she wanted to get a few of her friends and come to their party. He said that he didn't know if Jeff would be there, but that he would try to reach him.

When George Andrews, another Ram friend of Jeff's, told him about Stacy and asked him if he wanted to come to the outing Jeff agreed. He was excited to get to meet the girl who had written the letter.

The guys arrived and a few minutes went by before the introductions began. Jeff had already spotted the one he hoped was Stacy. His wish came true.

Stacy and Jeff began to date, they fell in love, and were married. Jeff says the first time he saw her, he had a sense she was the one he would marry and that God had truly picked her out for him.

"It wasn't until I chose God's purpose for my life that God revealed His plan for me. Making the team for the Los Angeles Rams was part of that plan, having all those Christian guys on the team was part of the plan, the friendships that were created along the way were in the plan, and meeting Stacy was also part of that plan" Jeff told me.

"God sees the big picture. He is a God of detail and has every step of our lives ordered," Jeff maintains.

❀ ❀ ❀

Delight yourself also in the LORD, and He shall give you the desires of your heart. . . . Trust also in Him, and He shall bring it to pass.

PSALM 37:4–5

DID I SHAVE MY LEGS FOR THIS?

Deana Carter's debut album *Did I Shave My Legs for This?* sold more than five million copies, and her single "Strawberry Wine" went to #1 on the Billboard charts and was named the Academy of Country Music's Single of the Year. Her second release, *Everything's Gonna Be Alright* is a vibrant collection of songs that picks up where *Legs* left off.

After her father, Fred Carter, a well-known Nashville session guitarist, received a kidney transplant that saved his life, Deana became passionate about urging people to sign donor cards. She is now a spokesperson for the National Kidney Foundation.

Deana called me on her way home from a doctor's appointment where she'd just been diagnosed with pneumonia. I asked her if she'd like to reschedule, but she didn't want to inconvenience me. Deana was considerate and caring and I found her to be endearing as well as a woman of principles and high integrity.

PRIOR TO BECOMING ONE OF THE MOST well-known female country music singers in the world, Deana Carter's life had been anything but platinum.

There seem to be three unspoken requirements for becoming

a country music singer, and Deana had managed to meet all three: she had worked as a waitress, worked for a temp service, and resided in a tiny run-down apartment while experiencing at least occasional car trouble.

In addition, she taught preschool, cleaned houses, and sold auto parts. In fact, for most of her climb to the top, Deana worked three and four jobs on a regular basis just to make ends meet.

Deana spent most of her life in Nashville and is close to her family. But when her grandparents passed away, her parents moved back to Louisiana where they were from originally.

Just before the Christmas holidays in 1996, Deana was close to signing her first record deal. She was doing everything within her power to finalize her contract with Capitol Records so she would have the money she needed to travel to Louisiana and spend the holidays with her family.

Unfortunately, record companies do very little business between the Thanksgiving and Christmas holidays. If contracts haven't been inked by the week before Christmas, the chances are slim to none that the completion will be facilitated until business resumes sometime after the New Year.

Undaunted by this fact and determined to do her best to make it happen, Deana persisted. She stopped by the offices and left phone messages for everyone involved in the negotiation process. No one was returning her calls. Certainly the thought, "Did I shave my legs for this?" must have crossed her mind, even before she recorded the song!

Her teaching job was in recess for the holidays. All of the full-time waitresses were pulling double shifts to make extra money for Christmas, so her part-time position had dwindled down to a no-time position until the first of the year. In addition, her house-cleaning clients had all gone out of town to visit their families.

Her only chance of getting the money to go home lay in executing her record contract. If that were to happen, she would receive a cash advance against royalties.

It was the 23rd of December and the offices were scheduled to close at noon on Christmas Eve. She knew that apart from her deal coming through, she had little hope of funding her trip to Louisiana.

Once again, she made her familiar round of phone calls to the record executives. And once again, no one returned her calls.

On Christmas Eve morning, one of the executives at Capitol called to let her know that they had been unable to complete all of her paperwork. They wouldn't be finalizing the contracts until after the holidays.

That night, she sat alone in her apartment eating her Christmas Eve dinner—a Cornish hen and Stove Top dressing. As she sat by herself, she became sad and extremely lonely for her family.

After dinner, Deana lay on her couch talking with her parents on the phone. They tried to be as upbeat as possible, but the reality of being apart for Christmas was making the cheery exchange somewhat difficult. Giving way to their disappointment of not being together, the phone call ended with everyone in tears. They said their good-byes and promised to talk again the next morning.

Still curled up on the couch. Deana gazed out the window and began to cry. Then she prayed, "God, you know I can't have anything for Christmas this year. I don't mean to be ungrateful for all I do have and sound so pitiful and everything, but could you please at least let it snow? Please, just let me wake up tomorrow and see just one or two snowflakes. That would be great!"

Then Deana cried herself to sleep.

On Christmas morning, she woke up around 7 A.M. She looked out the window to find huge snowflakes falling from the sky. The ground was covered with fresh, white, powdery snow.

As she recalled all of the Christmases that she had spent in Nashville, Deana couldn't remember ever having seen a white Christmas. God had made a special provision simply because one of His children had asked Him to.

That moment will forever be etched on Deana's heart. For her, the beautiful snowfall meant that during one of her loneliest times, she was being watched over.

Like most success stories, Deana suffered many delays and paid more than her fair share of dues on her journey to the top. But now she's riding the BIG wave. And in regard to the record-setting, chart-busting, and paramount accomplishments she's achieved so far, I'm certain the answer to the question is, "YES!" She definitely did *shave her legs for this!*

❀ ❀ ❀

Therefore humble yourselves under the mighty hand of God that He may exalt you in due time, casting all your cares upon Him, for He cares for you.

1 PETER 5:6–7

THEY THAT WAIT ON THE LORD

As a ten-year veteran animator for Walt Disney Animation, Nik Ranieri has many films to his credit, beginning with work on the tough-talking toddler, Baby Herman, and *Who Framed Roger Rabbit?*'s lead character, Roger Rabbit. He has brought many other characters to life including Ursula the Sea Witch in *The Little Mermaid*, Wilbur the Albatross in *The Rescuers Down Under*, the debonair Lumiere in *Beauty and the Beast*, the villainous Jafar in *Aladdin*, Meeko the mischievous raccoon in *Pocahontas*, and Hades the fast-talking, hot-headed villain in *Hercules*. Nik is currently working on the lead character for the next Disney animated feature film.

During our phone interview, Nik told me, "For most of my young adulthood, God has been sending life's lessons across my path for the sole purpose of teaching me patience and the rewards of waiting." But just like most Disney movies, Nik's story has a happy ending.

FROM AS FAR BACK AS HE CAN REMEMBER, Nik always wanted to have a career in art, but he wasn't sure exactly what area of art he would pursue. By the time he was ready to begin applying for colleges, he had decided that animation was perfectly suited to his artistic talents and pursuing it would result in the career of his dreams.

He learned about an animation course that really intrigued him and decided to apply for entrance into the program. Unfortunately, though, his grades weren't quite good enough and he was not accepted.

Instead, Nik was accepted into the Fundamental Arts program, which would expose him to a variety of art-related subjects. By doing well in this program, he would be eligible for the animation program the following year.

Nik was reluctant because he had no desire to study anything other than animation. There was, however, a small animation class that was part of the Fundamental Arts program, so he decided to give it a try. He excelled in animation and drawing, but failed the five other classes. The Director of Admissions not only refused to let him into the animation program, but also insisted that Nik retake the five classes he had failed, bring up his grades, and then reapply for the animation course.

Nik was emphatic with the administrator: "I can't take those courses again. They're useless. I don't want to learn how to do 'tie-dye.' I want to be an animator."

The administrator wouldn't budge. In fact, he told Nik it was just as well that he wasn't accepted into the course because he would probably never make it as an animator anyway.

Devastated, Nik took a year off. He began to question God, asking why He had led him to this animation class and allowed his hopes to grow, only to have them shot down.

"But what I learned is that God could see the whole picture. He was in the process of preparing me for the desires of my heart," Nik told me.

During his hiatus, Nik shot his own film and produced some commercials for a local television station. He took those same commercials back to the administration department at the school of animation and used them to demonstrate his capabilities. Nik was finally accepted into the college where he graduated three years later.

Within a month of graduation, Nik landed a job on an animated television series as an assistant animator. Within three months, he was promoted to an animator. The people who were his production assistants were the same people who had graduated the year he would have, had it not been for the delays.

What Nik didn't realize was that, until that particular year when the market finally opened up for animators, most of his coworkers had made a living driving cabs and working odd jobs. It was not until the year Nik graduated that the industry had started picking up.

Nik had a profound thought: *Wow, God knew more than I did!*

"All of the times I was crying out to Him, God knew the end of the story and that waiting would eventually allow me to experience His highest and best."

Nik continued in animation, moving from studio to studio, working on a variety of projects including TV specials and commercials. Some of the projects even utilized the very elaborate and time-consuming live-action/animation combination technique similar to the one in the movie *Who Framed Roger Rabbit?* Nik would later use. As he put it, "I was being prepared and totally set up for a major blessing!"

Nik was eventually hired as an "in-betweener" of animation on *Who Framed Roger Rabbit?,* where he was able to showcase his skills.

As a result, Nik was promoted and generously given many choice scenes in the film, most of which included the title character itself. After that, Nik was transferred to Los Angeles and was hired to animate various Disney characters in every Disney animated film to follow.

Nik tries to live having faith in God no matter what: "I've been through enough waiting in my life to know that when the delays come I can trust that God has my best interest at heart and when the waiting is complete and the time is right, the rewards will be great!"

❀ ❀ ❀

Those who wait on the LORD shall renew their strength;
they shall mount up with wings like eagles. They shall run
and not be weary, they shall walk and not faint.

ISAIAH 40:31

THE BODYGUARD

During his career as a bodyguard, Frank D'Amato has guarded such well-known bodies as Michael Jackson, Tiffany, Boyz 2 Men, New Kids on the Block, Ted Nugent, Kiss, INXS, royalty of all persuasions, and the list goes on.

When I met Frankie D by phone, I was entertained by his demeanor. In fact, because of his thick New York accent, at times it felt as though I was conversing with Rocky. One thing's for sure: Talking with Frankie D is anything but boring.

❀ ❀ ❀

A S A YOUNGSTER, FRANK D'AMATO accepted Christ as his Savior while watching a Jesus movie. He attended a non-denominational church and believed what his father had always told him, that someday when he died, he would see God. Unfortunately, Frank lived his life as he saw fit and never paid a great deal of attention to the ways of God.

As an adult, in addition to his duties as a bodyguard, Frank had a healthy sideline going on as a gangster. After being shot, having a heart attack, and suffering with a myriad of other health problems, Frank ended up being unable to work at all. He had come close to dying on at least four different occasions.

So Frank took a position as a bouncer at a prison. A riot broke out and Frank's back was badly injured. He dropped from 230 to 165 pounds. He was unable to work out. He had a heart problem. And he suffered from several other medical disorders that really affected the quality of his life.

As he was recuperating, Frank began reading a book called *Think Rich*, written by Napoleon Hill. He should have been able to read the book in one sitting, but he was so illiterate, it took him three months to complete. The sum of what he got out of the book was that God had a purpose for everyone's life.

Frank began to contemplate: "I wonder what my purpose was supposed to have been?"

So, he prayed a simple prayer: "God if you're really real, show me."

Around that time, Frank's wife was taking acting lessons. When Jackie, her acting coach, failed to show up for her class, she investigated the situation and found out that her coach's body had been severely crushed when a 150-pound door had fallen on top of her.

Frank and his wife went to see Jackie in the hospital and couldn't believe the list of critical injuries she had sustained. Yet within a very short time, they saw her again and she had been healed. It was a miracle.

Jackie was married to a modern-day prophet named Paul, who believed that the Lord could heal and deliver anyone of any infirmity. Frank had a desire to know God and to experience that same power in his own life, but he was skeptical of Paul and of any hidden motives he might have.

The more he thought about his own health problems, however, the more Frank leaned toward giving this prophet a shot at helping him. So, Frank decided to share his situation with Paul: "My wife has suffered with colitis for six and a half years. She has to adhere to a very strict diet. She can have no dairy products, nuts, or chocolate. And Paul, I really want to know God and believe that He is real, but I'm in terrible health and have almost died four times. I think God's trying to kill me!"

Paul smiled confidently and responded, "Frank, God's not trying to kill you. He wants you and your wife to have your health restored. God loves you, Frank. It's Satan who's trying to kill you."

Paul invited Frank and his wife to church and they agreed to go. Paul asked Frank to come up to the altar, where he began to tell him things in his life that he needed to change.

Frank sensed God telling him that he would see God's power come upon him and that he, too, would have healing in his hands. He was not to take any credit for performing any miracles himself, but was to always give God the glory.

During the service that followed, Frank's wife was completely healed of colitis. Her waist was reduced by about eight inches. Everyone in the service witnessed it. This was all new to Frank and he wanted to confirm for himself that her healing was real.

"We left church and went to Baskin Robbins for a hot fudge sundae, complete with chocolate syrup and nuts. Prior to that night, if she had eaten a sundae, she wouldn't have been able to leave the house for several days because of excruciating pain and an upset stomach. She ate the sundae and had no ill effects whatsoever."

Later that night, Frank had a dream where he saw his life flash before him and a host of people who were trying to be "wise guys" just like he had been. Then Frank saw a bright white light and Jesus appeared. Jesus told him that he was causing many people to go astray and that he needed to turn away from the life he had been living.

"I began to cry and told Jesus that I felt guilty and ashamed and knew that I deserved to go straight to hell. Jesus told me that He loved me and was going to restore me physically, spiritually, and financially."

Frank asked Jesus why He would want to do that, and Jesus responded by telling Frank that Frank was His son and that He loved him. He told Frank that he had been a leader for the devil and that he would now become a leader for Him.

At that point, Frank told Jesus that he would serve Him for all of his days.

About 10 A.M. the next day, a close friend of Frank's called him and said, "Hey Frankie, I was praying for you this morning and God told me He was going to fully restore you physically, spiritually, and financially."

Frank dropped the phone and began to run around his house. God had used his friend to confirm that his dream was truly from God.

Over time, all that had been lost was completely restored to Frank—physically spiritually, and financially.

Today, he is one of the most highly sought after bodyguards in the country and shares with everyone he meets how the power of God changed his life. And as promised, he gives God all of the glory.

The LORD is my light and my salvation. Whom then shall I fear? The LORD is the strength of my life; of whom shall I be afraid? When the wicked came against me to eat up my flesh, my enemies and foes stumbled and fell. Though an army may encamp against me, my heart shall not fear; though war may rise against me, in this I will be confident. One thing I have desired of the LORD and that I will seek. That I may dwell in the house of the LORD, all the days of my life.

PSALM 27:1-4

Now I'll Be Able to Worship Jesus Forever!

Scott Wesley Brown is an amazing songwriter, dynamic singer, inspirational worship leader, daring world missionary, and friend of God. His songs have been recorded by Sandi Patty, Amy Grant, Bruce Carroll, Pat Boone, The Imperials, Petra, and international opera star Placido Domingo.

For many years, and prior to the iron curtain coming down, Scott Wesley Brown's ministry, I CARE, smuggled musical instruments into third world counties where the church is being persecuted.

I first met Scott when he served as one of the judges for the songwriting competition at the Christian Artist Music Seminar. I consider him to be my brother and friend and was honored to hear his stories. I admire Scott's musical gifts, but beyond that, he is perhaps one of the most committed Christians I know. He is truly fearless.

O N ONE OF HIS TRIPS TO RUSSIA, it appeared that the KGB confiscated Scott's guitar at the airport. Scott had seen his guitar go onto the plane in Frankfurt, but it never came off of the plane in Moscow. He was devastated and wondered how he was going to perform his concerts without his instrument.

Scott looked all over Moscow for a music store that carried guitars. He was directed to stores that carried records, but no instruments and was never able to locate a guitar.

When Scott arrived at the first church to which he had been invited, he stood at the back of the church, talking with the pastor and some of the elders.

They asked him if he would sing.

Scott told them he would love to accommodate them, but that his guitar had been confiscated and he had nothing to play. He asked the pastor if there was any way to locate a guitar.

The pastor looked disheartened and humbly expressed to Scott that finding a guitar would be a very difficult task. The pastor, determined to try, consulted with some of the others. Soon, they all scattered in different directions.

Within a short time, the pastor came back to Scott and said they had located a boy who had a guitar. They had sent the boy to his flat to fetch it and he would return with it shortly.

About twenty minutes later, the young man returned to the church. He was sweaty, totally out of breath, and carried a soiled duffel bag that was ripped and torn. In a seemingly reluctant manner, he opened up the bag, reached in, and pulled out the guitar.

Never had Scott seen an instrument in such ill repair. A guitar is supposed to have one hole in its center, but this guitar had several holes. The neck was twisted and the strings were about an inch off of the neck.

Scott noticed that when he first picked up the guitar, the young man had a somewhat fearful look on his face. It was obvious that his guitar meant a lot to him. Scott wanted to assure him that he knew how to play the guitar so he started doing a little picking and strumming to establish a comfort level with the young man.

The young man was not comforted. He glared at Scott and blurted out something in Russian that Scott wasn't able to understand.

Scott asked the pastor to tell him what the young man had said. The pastor told Scott that the boy didn't want him to play so hard because it had taken him a year to save up for new strings.

Scott compassionately thought to himself, *a whole year*. The pastor explained to Scott that the boy felt incredibly blessed to have an instrument at all. Instruments were luxuries to these churches.

Then Scott realized he had about a dozen packs of guitar strings in his knapsack. He retrieved the strings and asked the pastor how to say "gift" in Russian.

Scott handed the strings to the boy and said the Russian word for gift. At first, the boy wouldn't take them. He just stared at Scott in disbelief. But Scott kept repeating the word gift over and over again.

Finally, the boy took the strings. He looked at Scott, then at the strings. Then he began to jump up and down, blurting out something else in Russian, each sentence ending in "Hallelujah!"

Again, Scott asked the pastor to interpret. The pastor relayed to Scott that the boy was saying, "Never have I seen so many guitar strings! Now I'll be able to worship Jesus forever. Hallelujah!"

Scott was blown away by how grateful the boy was. The boy wasn't just thinking about having a lot of strings or that he'd never run out. He wasn't thinking that he could sell them on the black market. He wasn't even thinking that he was now the coolest guy on the block. His whole focus was in worshipping Jesus.

On Scott's plane ride home, he looked at Ephesians 4:12 which talks about the fact that we've all been given various gifts, "for the equipping of the saints for the work of the ministry, for the edifying of the body of Christ."

The word equipping kept bubbling up in Scott's spirit and eventually developed into a ministry.

I CARE now goes into third world countries, not only equipping them with instruments, but also equipping them with encouragement and instruction in how to play an instrument and how to worship through music.

Three months following that trip, Scott's guitar did come back to him in America and he learned that the KGB had, in fact, taken it. On his next trip over to Eastern Europe, he took that same guitar with him and ended up giving it away because he realized how desperately the churches needed instruments.

Scott has received many blessings since then. He stood with his East German brothers and sisters as the Berlin Wall came down. In 1989, he performed at the first publicly promoted Christian concert, attended by over fifteen thousand people. At that event, over two thousand people joined the family of Christ.

When he takes a team of musicians into a country to do concerts and to minister, they now leave all of the instruments they bring with them. As a result, Scott has taken over one hundred musicians on trips to the mission field and has provided hundreds of instruments to musicians and missionaries in third world and restricted access countries.

Through his efforts, there are children of God throughout the whole earth who have been given the instruments they need to "be able to worship Jesus forever!"

❁ ❁ ❁

Give to the LORD the glory due His name: worship the LORD in the beauty of holiness.

PSALM 29:2

LOST & FOUND

Chloe was one of the best personal assistants Babbie Mason has ever had. She was efficient, personable, and treated everyone with courtesy and respect.

One of the most interesting things in Chloe's background is that in addition to her administrative skills, she is an incredible dancer and at one time was a dancer for the Atlanta Hawks basketball team. Chloe is certainly a woman of many diverse talents.

When Babbie conveyed this story to me, I was moved.

YEARS BEFORE CHLOE CAME TO WORK FOR BABBIE, she had been engaged to her high school sweetheart, Brian. When they became engaged, he had given her a modest diamond ring, and it was dear to Chloe. Brian meant the world to her and the ring he gave her served as a constant reminder of their love for each other.

After going through premarital counseling, and although they had known each other for years, Brian and Chloe decided that they were too young and immature to get married. There were just too many major differences to work through, so they put their engagement on hold and eventually decided to break up. Brian told Chloe he wanted her to keep the ring, and they parted as friends.

Shortly after that, Brian decided to move from Georgia to

California. Meanwhile Chloe took a job in Atlanta and was also able to utilize her dancing skills by being a cheerleader for the Atlanta Hawks basketball team.

She joined a wonderful church and became involved in ministering to the homeless people in the inner city. She helped prepare food in the soup kitchen, helped gather clothes, and assisted them in finding work. She also conducted a Bible study and led many of them to the Lord.

It was while she was there that she met a couple named Edgar and Selma Hawkins. Edgar and Selma were mentally challenged, but were always willing to do anything they were instructed to do.

Autumn was approaching and the temperatures were beginning to drop. Chloe noticed that Edgar and Selma continued to wear summer clothes and that neither of them had a winter coat. They were living in a shelter and barely had enough food to eat. Chloe knew they didn't have money to buy what they needed. She wanted to help them, but she didn't have any extra money either.

Then she remembered her engagement ring. It had been given to her as a symbol of love. What better way to love Edgar and Selma than to pawn her ring and give them the money so that they could buy winter coats?

The next day when Chloe arrived at the shelter, she informed Edgar and Selma of her intentions. They began to cry and told Chloe that her gesture was an answer to their prayers.

They all got into Chloe's car and went farther into the inner city to the pawnshop. They saw homeless people on every street corner begging for change. Scantily clad prostitutes paced up and down the sidewalks, crushing discarded hypodermics with their platform shoes. Unattended children darted across busy intersections looking for patches of grass to play on. Other children smoked marijuana and carried their babies on their hips. Loud music blasted from the windows of roach-invested apartment buildings, and buses dropped off passengers as they returned to this place they called home.

As Chloe, Edgar, and Selma exited the car, they walked briskly and cautiously into the pawnshop. Chloe pawned her ring and gave the money to Edgar and Selma. The three then drove back to a thrift shop, where they purchased their new winter coats and then Chloe dropped them off at the shelter.

Eight years later, Chloe went to the West Coast to visit her family. While there, she bumped into her former fiancé, Brian, at a restaurant. They began to talk about old times and quickly realized that they were still in love. During the years that they had been apart, they both had dated other people and each had come close to getting married. In each case, however, things had never worked out.

Chloe and Brian now realized that they had always been meant for each other, but they had just been too young before. Being older and wiser, this was their time.

They began a long distance relationship and ran up huge phone bills. They became certain that marriage was God's plan, so they set a date. Chloe was moving to California.

The next Sunday, Chloe went to church and told Edgar and Selma the good news of her pending wedding. She had become good friends with them and had been ministering to them through the years. After church, they all went out to lunch together so that Chloe could tell them goodbye.

During lunch, Chloe asked Edgar and Selma if they remembered the location of the pawnshop where they'd taken her ring eight years earlier. If so, did they think her ring would still be there? Edgar quickly responded that he remembered exactly where the shop was and suggested they all go down first thing Monday morning to see if they still had the ring.

As they entered the pawnshop, Chloe asked a woman about the ring.

The woman replied, "Do you have any identification?"

Chloe explained that it had been eight years.

"Well, do you remember the date you brought it in?"

Chloe didn't remember the date, but she did remember the month, because she knew it was beginning to get cold.

The woman asked Chloe for her driver's license and told her that they could match up her merchandise with the driver's license number. A match was made and it was determined that the ring was still there. The only problem was that her ring was displayed in a case with two thousand other diamond rings.

The search began. After a few hours, the woman found Chloe's ring, tucked away in the same box she had left it in eight years before.

Chloe let out a burst of joy and said, "I don't care how much it costs. It's mine, it's been lost, and I've come to redeem it."

She bought it back and went home to phone Brian with the news. They rejoiced together over Chloe's success in being able to reclaim something that had such sentimental value for both of them.

They were married in December of 1998 and now live in California.

Being a teacher at heart, Babbie concluded Chloe's story the following way: "This story reminds us of our position of being separated from God, our circumstances of hopelessness and our situation as sinners when Christ came to redeem us. We were all lost in the dregs of life and disregarding what it would cost to redeem us, Jesus paid the price to get us back!"

❋ ❋ ❋

Behold what manner of love the Father has bestowed on us, that we should be called the children of God!

1 JOHN 3:1

You've Got a Friend

Dr. Clifton Taulbert is the acclaimed speaker and author of *Once Upon A Time When We Were Colored, Watching Our Crops Come In,* and *Eight Habits of the Heart.* He was also nominated for a Pulitzer Prize for *The Last Train North.*

My interview with Dr. Taulbert took place by phone as he awaited the arrival of out of town family members who were expected for the Christmas holidays. A few months after our interview, I met Dr. Taulbert at one of his speaking engagements and learned that not only does he have the gift of writing, but also for teaching.

There are many lessons to be learned from his sad, but wonderful story.

※ ※ ※

THE PULITZER PRIZE NOMINATION for *The Last Train North* was not enough. His success as the writer of the American classic *Once Upon A Time When We Were Colored* was not enough. In fact, nothing would be enough to sustain him when in 1994, Clifton and his wife suffered the loss of their seven-year-old daughter to sickle cell anemia.

Clifton experienced a myriad of emotions, from grief to depression to anger. He questioned God, as well as his faith in God. He longed for a friend who could listen to him, cry with him, and allow him to question the *why* of his tragedy.

About four months after his daughter's death, Clifton and his wife got up one morning and found that their old refrigerator, which had been repaired time and time again, had permanently expired. After getting the opinions of two service people, the refrigerator's final rights were read. It was not cooling. It would not make ice. Even adding Freon wouldn't remedy the situation.

Following dinner that evening, Dr. and Mrs. Taulbert set out for the neighborhood Sears store. They had pre-determined the model they wanted to purchase but upon arriving at Sears, they were disappointed to learn that this store was out of the particular model they wanted. So the salesclerk called another Sears that was located all the way across town. Although it was very close to closing time and the drive to the store was substantial, the salesclerk at the second Sears store said he would be glad to wait on the Taulberts.

Upon arrival, they learned that the salesclerk, Perry Shockley, was a well-known basketball coach who had come to Tulsa to go to Bible school and was only selling appliances part time. He had the refrigerator they wanted, so they put down a deposit and set up the delivery date.

An instant rapport developed between Clifton and Perry, but Clifton couldn't really say why. Perry was an athlete and Clifton was a writer. Perry was a white guy and Clifton was black. It didn't seem like they had all that much in common, but Clifton still knew he wanted to get to know Perry.

Clifton and his wife returned home so they could be there when their old refrigerator was picked up. But when they got there, much to their amazement, the old refrigerator was working perfectly.

Clifton called Perry, apologized, and let him know they would not need the new refrigerator after all. He returned to the store to get his down payment back and to undo the paperwork. It was during that visit that Clifton discovered what the two had in common: They were both trying to build their relationships with the Lord.

They began to talk as if they had been friends for all of their lives. Clifton invited Perry to dine with his friends and family; they began to build camaraderie to the point where both of them felt comfortable sharing their innermost hopes and dreams.

They opened up a free-flowing and honest communication about Jesus. They discussed whether or not He would really "hang in there" through everything. After spending time seeking the answer to their question, their conclusion was an emphatic *Yes!* Throughout the good times, as well as the challenges in life, Jesus never leaves or forsakes those He loves.

The more Clifton and Perry prayed and studied together, the deeper they fell in love with God. Perry shared with Cliff about various mission trips he'd taken to Russia and Africa. He said that although he loved basketball and coaching with all his heart, he now got as excited over someone coming to know the Lord as he used to get when he coached a basketball game.

That a regular guy could be this energized about knowing Jesus opened Clifton's heart and allowed God to begin healing the wounds he had suffered when he lost his little girl.

Through having meals together, taking walks, and having deep conversations and debates, Cliff and Perry both received what they needed. They had developed the ability to laugh, talk, and cry freely, having grown to respect and trust each other.

"God allowed my refrigerator to go on the blink and sent me all the way across town to meet Perry, the friend I needed. God then restored my refrigerator so that I would realize that the Lord orchestrates whatever He has to in order to give His children whatever we need!"

Clifton and Perry are still best friends and the refrigerator lasted two and a half more years.

❀ ❀ ❀

Be anxious for nothing but in everything by prayer and supplication, with thanksgiving, let your requests be known to God; and the peace of God which surpasses all understanding, will guard your hearts and minds through Christ Jesus.

PHILIPPIANS 4:6–7

PURE GOLD

A former member of the Indianapolis Colts and currently a cornerback for the Atlanta Falcons, where in 1999 he played in the Super Bowl, Ray Buchanan has seen great success in his young career. The Ray Buchanan Football Camp he founded benefits the Make-A-Wish Foundation and the Boys and Girls Clubs of America, stressing a strong "stay in school, stay away from drugs" message. Ray has also recently completed work on a new CD of inspirational songs, including a mixture of jazz, soft ballads, and rap, and is a frequent speaker at youth gatherings across the country. He lives in the Atlanta area with his wife, Sheree, and three children—Destinee´ who is seven, Ray Jr. who is five, and Baylen who is nine months.

I called Ray on his cell phone at a pre-arranged time and someone on the other end whispered, "Hello?"

"Ray?" I said, wondering exactly what was going on.

"Donna, this isn't Ray. I'm one of his friends. But he asked me to tell you to call back in twenty minutes. He's in the middle of talking to three hundred kids at a high school and it's going a little longer than he anticipated."

"No problem, glad to do it," I responded.

Twenty minutes later when I reached Ray as he drove home, he apologized and told me how much he appreciated that I was able to call him back. Such humility . . . how refreshing! I found in speaking with Ray that not only does he have a heart for God and his family, but he really has a heart for helping kids with making good choices and staying on the right path. Ray has a desire and a passion to guide young people down the best and most productive roads in life.

❀ ❀ ❀

AT THE AGE OF TWELVE, Ray accepted Jesus as his Savior. But that day, walking down the aisle of his church was not much more than a verbal commitment. A deeper commitment would come later.

Earning a full scholarship, Ray attended the University of Louisville where, with each play, he began carving out a legacy for his future. While in school, he experienced all of the regular temptations, but because he had a conscience and due to his religious upbringing, he managed to make it through successfully.

Upon graduation, the Indianapolis Colts, with whom he hoped to spend his entire career, drafted him. He had made a big name for himself there and had all of the elements in place to become a superstar.

Along with becoming an NFL player came fame and more money than he'd ever seen in his life. As a result he found himself wanting material possessions. Houses, cars, clothes, expensive restaurants, dream vacations—Ray had it all and was basking in all of it.

In 1996, however, Ray became convicted of his extravagance and in a simple prayer asked God to become the Lord of his life. He knew that he had been saved as a child, but now he wanted God to live through him. He wanted everything he did to honor and glorify Jesus.

Shortly after Ray's decision to surrender to the Lordship of Christ, he was injured by one of his own players in a game against the New York Jets. Ray was hit in the thigh. What would have normally been considered a thigh bruise had blown up to be almost as large as his chest by that evening.

The doctors had never seen anything like it before and had no idea how to diagnosis Ray's injury or what to do to repair it. They put him on pain medication and instructed him to keep his leg iced. To Ray, it felt like a migraine headache over his entire leg. The pain was excruciating.

For the next three weeks, Ray spent a lot of time studying the Bible and praying. He sensed that God had allowed this injury to make certain that He and Ray would have time to get to know each other in a more intimate way. Ray looked at this time as an opportunity for spiritual growth: "I wondered if my injury would ever heal and if I would ever get back to playing the game I loved so much. The doctors had still been unable to come up with how to treat my leg, so I decided I would put my entire faith and trust in the God I claimed to love and serve."

Ray decided that even if he could never play again, he would continue to love the Lord with all of his heart and would follow Him all the days of his life. Ray relays his turning point: "One evening, the Lord came to me in a vision. It felt very dream-like—in my peripheral vision, all the sights and sounds around me in the room were in place."

"In this dream, God told me that the 'pinch' on my thigh was nothing. What I was experiencing was only a glimpse of where I would have been headed if I had not come to the decision to turn my life over to God."

Ray got down on his knees and cried out, "God, I don't even care about my leg. I just want to know You. I love You, God, and I want to spend forever with You. I want to serve You and please You and honor You with my life."

"God told me that everything was going to be all right!"

The next morning, Ray awakened full of the joy and peace of the Lord. Nothing could steal his joy and everyone around Ray could detect that something had happened to cause this change in attitude.

The doctors told Ray they knew he was religious, but that his injury was substantial and he shouldn't get his hopes up. They were going to have to perform exploratory surgery to investigate why his injury was not healing. Ray told them to do what they needed to do. "God is going to use you to help me, but God already assured me that everything would turn out fine."

The surgery revealed a hematoma between his muscles, causing the muscles to be unable to connect. The doctors used ultrasound and needles to extract it.

Less than a week after surgery, Ray was back out on the field and helped his team play against the Kansas City Chiefs which resulted in them making it to the Division play-offs.

After going through this entire ordeal, Ray was traded to the Atlanta Falcons. He didn't understand why God had planted him with this particular team because he had planned to spend his career in Indianapolis.

But Ray trusted God.

After a year of playing with the Falcons, and for the first time in Falcon history, the team went to the Super Bowl in 1999. Once again Ray was part of a winning team.

❀ ❀ ❀

But He knows the way that I take; when He has tested me I shall come forth as gold. My foot has held fast to His steps; I have kept His way and have not turned aside. I have not departed from the commandment of His lips; I have treasured the words of His mouth more than my necessary food.

JOB 23:10–12

BLIND TRUST

Greg Nelson is a premier songwriter and an award-winning record producer. He has worked with artists such as Sandi Patty, Larnelle Harris, Scott Wesley Brown, Steve Green, and Sheila Walsh. He has created many highly successful musical works including *Le Voyage, Saviour, The Passion,* and *Emmanuel,* featuring Amy Grant, Michael W. Smith, Point of Grace, Jaci Velesquez, Larnelle Harris, Twila Paris, Wayne Watson, and many others. He is currently developing a feature film project based on the book *Pilgrim's Progress.*

Greg was the producer with whom I signed my first song publishing deal. I consider him to be my brother and friend and have learned much of what I know about songwriting by studying his works.

Although I could have done his interview by phone, I decided to drive to Nashville and see him live and up close. Whenever we get together, I can always be assured of three things: great stories, an excellent lunch, and so much laughter that the following day my stomach always feels like I've done at least ten-thousand sit-ups!

❀ ❀ ❀

IN THE FALL OF 1987, record producer Greg Nelson boarded a plane in Los Angeles bound for his home in Nashville, Tennessee. He had just completed a Christmas record for Evie, a contemporary Christian artist.

After landing and claiming his luggage, he retrieved his car and headed toward his house. During the drive home, he began to feel like he had something in his eyes. The further he drove, the more distracting the situation with his eyes became.

By the time he got home, the irritation in his eyes was intense. He flushed them out with water and then tried washing them with eyewash. Nothing seemed to remove the obstruction or ease the discomfort, so he decided to get some sleep and hoped the problem would resolve itself by the next morning.

The next day, the irritation was even worse. It increased over the next several days until he couldn't see out of either eye very well. So Greg called his doctor, and his wife, Pam, drove him to the appointment.

Following an examination, his family physician immediately scheduled Greg to see a specialist. The specialist gave him a steroid shot directly into each eye. Not only were the shots extremely painful, but they produced no results.

So then Greg went to Vanderbilt Hospital, where an entire battery of tests was implemented. The specialists there were puzzled as to the etiology of the trauma, but they were able to determine that there was severe scarring over the center of vision in both of his eyes. By this time, Greg could not even see the faces of his wife or children.

However, being the eternal optimist that he is, he held to the hope that his impending blindness was only temporary. People everywhere were praying for him, but it seemed the more they prayed, the worse he got.

At that point, Greg was beginning to realize the seriousness of his condition—he was blind. He sold his car. His wife drove him to and from work, and his assistant read all of his mail to him.

The clients for whom he had produced records were understanding and willing to stick with him. He found himself thanking God that it was his eyes and not his ears that had been affected. At least he was still able to produce records.

Dealing with the reality of Greg's loss was difficult for everyone who knew and loved him. But Greg tried to live just one day at a time, still hoping that something would change.

A year later, Greg was about to return to Anderson, Indiana, to work on another record with Christian recording artist Sandi Patty. Semi-resigned to the fact that his vision might never improve, however, Greg decided that after completing this project, he was going to enroll in Braille school so that he could learn how to read.

The week before going to Anderson, Greg's church held a healing service for him. They anointed him with oil and prayed over him, asking that God perform a miracle to restore his sight. This was the first time his church had ever embarked on a service of this type.

Then Greg traveled to Anderson and began working on Sandi's new project. One day, while Sandi was in the vocal booth, Greg was seated in the control room of the studio. Just as Greg cued Sandi, he thought he saw her hands moving. Greg wondered, had his imagination gone wild, or could it be that he wanted so much to see that he was hallucinating?

"Very bizarre!" he thought to himself. He decided not to say anything to anyone.

The next day, he continued to think that he was actually seeing certain things. He had been in this particular studio hundreds of times, however, and he convinced himself that he was only remembering the room.

Upon returning to Nashville, Greg immediately went to the doctor. The doctor examined his eyes and asked Greg what church he went to.

The doctor went on to tell Greg that although he couldn't explain it, the scar tissue was going away on his left eye. He wasn't imagining anything. He could see! The doctor further explained that scar tissue doesn't just go away by itself. What Greg was experiencing was beyond medical explanation.

Greg says he has no idea why God allowed him to become blind for a year or why when God did decide to heal him, He only restored the vision in his left eye. But I'll never forget when Greg called to tell me how he once again saw the faces of his wife and children. It was a moment of celebration.

As Greg tells it, "The experience that God entrusted to me taught me to rest in God's plan and to be content in all things, even when I didn't know how the story would end. I also learned that the only real trust is blind trust because it creates in us a state of complete abandonment to a tender and loving God."

For My thoughts are not your thoughts nor are your ways My ways. For as the heavens are higher than the earth, so are My ways higher than your ways and My thoughts than your thoughts.

ISAIAH 55:8–9

VERN

Vern Stewart has served in the United States Navy, acting as the assistant to her chaplain. I met her when she came to the Women's Crisis Pregnancy Center. I know her story well because I witnessed it as it unfolded. Vern is a walking miracle and a testament to the power of God to change a willing heart.

THE GIRL SAT IN A LATE-YEAR-MODEL FORD at the edge of the church parking lot. Jeannie, a social worker and one of the last members to be leaving the church that Sunday, noticed the lone car with the girl sitting in the driver's seat. She approached the car and spoke into the slightly cracked window.

"Can I help you?" Jeannie asked.

The girl looked to be in her early twenties. She had light brown hair, piercing blue eyes, and pasty, white skin.

She rolled the window halfway down and turned toward Jeannie, but kept her eyes averted. Then she spoke with the eerie voice of a five-year-old child.

"Yes, maybe you can help me. I think I may be pregnant."

"Could I take you to lunch? We could talk about it," Jeannie replied.

The girl nodded affirmatively.

Her name was Vern. Jeannie learned that throughout her childhood, beginning as early as four years old, she had been raped by many of her family friends and relatives. Now she thought she might be pregnant with her father's child.

A pregnancy test confirmed her suspicions.

Over the next few weeks, Paula, who was director of the local Women's Crisis Pregnancy Center, scheduled several appointments with psychologists to evaluate Vern. While driving her to and from appointments, Paula tried to instigate conversation and learned small pieces of information to a very large and ugly puzzle. The abuse was too horrific to imagine.

All of the doctors concluded that the coping mechanisms Vern had developed to deal with the criminal acts inflicted upon her young life had made her a paranoid schizophrenic and, most probably, emotionally and mentally retarded. That was why she spoke in such an infantile voice. A person who has undergone severe trauma often reverts to the age at which they were originally abused.

The recommendation was to institutionalize her, but Paula wasn't ready to accept that sentence for Vern.

One of the things Paula had learned during her talks with Vern was that she had never had a doll or a teddy bear. In fact, she had never had a birthday party—no cake, no presents, and no recognition of her existence. Perhaps that had made it easier for her perpetrators to abuse her.

So a few people from the center got together and decided to change all of that. Many of the volunteers at the clinic had now met Vern and loved her. One day a group gathered at the Varsity, one of Vern's favorite places to eat. She was presented with a beautifully decorated birthday cake and presents galore. She was given Precious Moments dolls, several teddy bears, and a Precious Moments Bible. She seemed overwhelmed that so many people cared about her.

Vern moved into the Home for Unwed Mothers that was affiliated with the Women's Crisis Pregnancy Center. There, she attended Bible studies, ate meals with the other girls, and began to show some signs of emotional improvement. But within weeks of moving in, Vern had a miscarriage. This meant she was no longer eligible to live there and would have to return home.

Paula had another idea. There were several small apartments on the same property, which belonged to the home. Vern could move into one of them, and Paula would assign her some part-time duties, thereby allowing her to stay there. Vern was pleased with the suggestion.

Although Vern seemed to be doing well, eventually the nightmares and the memories were more than she could stand. She gave up hope of ever being able to live without the continuous torment.

She decided the only escape was to kill herself. One night, she gathered up her dolls, her teddy bears, and her Bible and placed them on the front seat of her car. Then she got into her car, which was parked in the garage at her apartment.

With the garage door closed and a sock stuffed into the exhaust, she neatly placed the note she had written to her new friends and surrogate family on the dashboard:

Dear Everybody,

You have been so kind to me. I love you all, but I keep having nightmares. The memories I have make it impossible for me to eat or sleep or hold down a job. It's all I ever think about. I am forever trapped. I just want to go be with Jesus.
Love,

Vern

Then she closed her eyes, anticipating her arrival in heaven.

But God had a different plan for Vern. The next morning, the sun peaked through a small window at the top of the garage. The light in Vern's face awakened her.

What? How could this be? she thought. She was still a living, breathing inhabitant of planet earth.

At first she couldn't figure out what had happened, but then the reality of God's tender hand brought her to tears. The gas gauge was on empty. Shortly after she slipped off to sleep, her car had run out of gas. God had intervened. Her plan was not His.

A couple of years later as I was having coffee with Paula, the phone rang around 10 P.M. Paula picked up the receiver, then squealed with elation. It was Vern. She was in the Navy and was stationed in California.

She was in the Navy? With thousands of men? Men who up unitl now she had been afraid of because of her past experiences?

Vern recounted to us how one night while reading her Precious Moments Bible, she had been struck by the way Jesus had cast demons out of a possessed man: "I began to call on God, telling Him that if He could do that for the man in the Bible, I saw no reason why He couldn't do the same thing for me—to cast out all the nightmares and bad memories that tortured me for so long. And guess what? That's exactly what He did. The memories and nightmares were cast out and I was set free!"

When she took her entrance exam for the Navy, she made one of the highest scores ever. This formerly paranoid-schizophrenic, slightly mentally and emotionally retarded girl tested as a borderline genius.

Her job assignment was working in the kitchen, and she had just won a trip to New York to study in the school of culinary art. She was also an assistant to the chaplain and was happy to tell her story to anyone who ever dared to doubt the power of prayer, love, and hope.

❀ ❀ ❀

And the LORD restored Job's losses when he prayed for his friends. Indeed the LORD gave Job twice as much as he had before.

JOB 42:10

85

HIS EYE IS ON
THE SPARROW

With six recorded albums and ten number one radio hits to her credit, Cindy Morgan is one of the top contemporary Christian female vocalists in the country today. As a songwriter, she has had her songs recorded by noted artists like Sandi Patty, Michael English, and BeBe Winans.

In addition to performing on her own records, Cindy has toured with and sung on the recordings for *The Young Messiah* and *My Utmost for His Highest*

Cindy and I met eight years ago when we were both panelists for an ASCAP workshop. We have since written together and became bonded even more when our dads passed away within four months of each other.

One of our song collaborations called "Live In the Moment" was inspired by the words of Celine Dion and we're hopeful it will be recorded in the very near future!

I N 1996, THE *LISTEN* TOUR, named for her fifth record, was full tilt. After completing numerous dates on the East Coast and in Middle America, Cindy, her band, and her crew headed to California for the West Coast leg of the tour.

Since Cindy was one of America's top contemporary Christian

artists, her new record was doing exceptionally well in sales, as well as in radio airplay. That was all well and good, but her favorite part of touring was just getting to sing and meet the fans.

They arrived from L.A. with their caravan of RV's for their first date in the Sacramento area. While backstage at this particular venue, Cindy began to unpack her clothes and found a mass of wrinkles in the black silk dress she planned on wearing. Realizing that the wrinkles were not going to steam out, she found herself in desperate need of an iron.

Cindy hated to bother the promoter. She knew he had his hands full trying to oversee the unloading and set-up of equipment, lights, and sound. But she realized that if they didn't have an iron there at the church, someone would have to go off campus and get one. She resisted having to put any additional burden on anyone, but convinced that she had no other alternative, Cindy called the promoter.

One of the women working for the promoter knew a staff member who would loan them his iron, but they'd have to go to his house to pick it up.

So the woman went over to the staff member's home and, thinking no one was at home, she used the key he'd given her to get into the house. She walked in, following the instructions she'd been given, and proceeded upstairs to retrieve the iron from a hall closet.

Just as she was about to reach the closet, she passed a bedroom where something out of her peripheral vision caught her attention. Inside the bedroom was the fifteen-year-old daughter of the staff member. She had a gun to her head and was about to take her own life.

Quickly, but calmly, the woman began to talk to the troubled teen. During their conversation, she learned that she was feeling overwhelmed over a number of issues going on in her life. She had not felt at liberty to discuss any of these situations with her parents or peers and had concluded that the only solution was suicide.

The woman assured her that this was not the answer. They talked until the girl calmed down enough to give her the gun. They prayed together and the girl came back to the church with her, where they began the process of getting her the help she needed.

It wasn't until after the concert that the promoter told Cindy what had happened. She was amazed and thankful for a wrinkled dress that required an iron.

One hundred sixty times a year, Cindy Morgan stands before audiences across the world and proclaims the good news of Jesus Christ through her music. Her goal in doing it is to offer people the love, hope, and peace that can be found in a relationship with the true and living God. On this day, Cindy played a part of saving the life of a teenager without hitting the first note. Cindy summarizes the situation this way, "God intervened in such an unusual way to reach out to a girl who was confused and in pain. Quite simply to rescue a life, He wrinkled a dress. What a profound reminder that if *His eye is on the sparrow, then I know He watches me.*"

❀ ❀ ❀

O LORD, You have searched me and known me. You know my sitting down and my rising up; You understand my thought afar off. You comprehend my path and my lying down, And you are acquainted with all my ways. For there is not a word on my tongue, but behold, O LORD, You know it altogether. You have hedged me behind and before, and laid Your hand upon me. Such knowledge is too wonderful for me; it is too high, I cannot attain it.

PSALM 139:1–6

THE REAL PRISONERS

Dr. Bill Bright is the president of Campus Crusade for Christ. Over the past fifty years, Dr. Bright has had many moving experiences as he has tried to help people in their quest for peace with God and for meaning and purpose in their lives.

Because of Dr. Bright's strenuous travel schedule, he was unable to give me an interview. However, he faxed me the following story and I welcomed his generous gesture and am honored to have his contribution.

SOME YEARS AGO, DR. BRIGHT was invited by the warden to speak to the inmates of the Federal Penitentiary in Atlanta, Georgia, one of the most infamous high-security prisons in America at that time. It was a place where prisoners who had committed major crimes, such as murder, were incarcerated. Some of the Campus Crusade staff members and volunteers had been working with hundreds of inmates and several of the inmates had become Christians.

When Dr. Bright arrived at the penitentiary assembly room, several inmates rushed over to embrace him, calling him "brother." They told him how much they had been helped by hearing his messages on tape and by reading his books. They also shared how much the Campus Crusade staff had helped them.

Before Dr. Bright spoke, some of the inmates stood and gave testimony of how they had been forgiven by God through faith in Christ's death on the cross and His resurrection. One man spoke of how he had murdered five people. Another three. Others had committed similar crimes. They told of how they had come to the prison full of hate and fear. Then they met Jesus and were transformed.

Tears streamed down his face as Dr. Bright listened to these testimonies of God's forgiveness, grace, goodness, and love. Again and again, inmates said, "I'm glad I'm here in this prison. If I had not been sent here, I would not know Christ, and I would probably be dead because of my life of crime."

These prisoners—these men behind bars—had experienced the wonder of God's eternal pardon from their sins. They had received peace of heart and mind. They were experiencing purpose and meaning for their lives, and they had been given power to be different, even in their prison cells.

Sitting there, Dr. Bright's mind raced across the continent to Hollywood, California, where just two nights prior, he had been privileged to be a guest at a large banquet of Hollywood personalities who had gathered to honor one of their own. Many of them were famous movie stars, producers, directors, or entertainers from all over the world.

He sat between a man who had been one of the great actors of our country for more than thirty years and the daughter of one of the founders of the Hollywood industry, the wife of a famous actor. Dr. Bright had barely taken his seat when the woman began telling him how miserable she was and how she was thinking about committing suicide. She said that she had nothing to live for. Her little dog, the most prized, beloved possession of her life, had died the day before and she was devastated.

She lived in a palatial mansion. She was world-famous. She had a great fortune at her disposal. And she felt she had nothing to live for.

When Dr. Bright shared the most joyful news of Christ's love for her through a little booklet, The Four Spiritual Laws, he saw a dramatic change in her countenance. She seemed overwhelmed to learn that God loved her and had a wonderful plan for her life. She asked if she could keep the booklet, stating that its content was so wonderful that she wanted to read it over and over again.

He then turned to the man on his left—an actor known to most Americans. He was inebriated. Dr. Bright tried to initiate a conversation by speaking to him of his work with students. The actor responded angrily saying, "Why waste your time on students? They're just a bunch of hotheaded radicals. Why doesn't someone work with older people?"

The man began to sob and continued, "Why doesn't somebody work with people like me? I need help!"

Dr. Bright was able to help that dear man. Later, he accepted Jesus as his Savior and was baptized in one of the larger churches in southern California.

Dr. Bright was overwhelmed with the contrast of these different scenarios. He thought of the people with wealth, fame, and power in Hollywood. They thought they were free, but they were actually in prison (imprisoned by their own selfish desires and fleshly pursuits of materialism and fame).

Then Dr. Bright thought of the men in the federal penitentiary who were free, even though they would never leave those gray, bleak prison walls. They were still free, happy, rejoicing and giving thanks to their Savior.

God's pardon, peace, purpose and power are available to everyone who by faith places their trust in the free gift of salvation through Jesus Christ. Through Campus Crusade for Christ International, Dr. Bill Bright has spent his entire life trying to make sure that everyone is given the opportunity to accept this wonderful gift!

❀ ❀ ❀

DONNA I. DOUGLAS

For the love of Christ compels us, because we judge thus:
that if One died for all, then all died; and He died for all,
that those who live should no longer live for themselves, but
for Him who died for them and rose again. Therefore, if
anyone be in Christ, he is a new creation; old things have
passed away; behold, all things have become new.

2 CORINTHIANS 5:14–15, 17

BIRD DOG

Sarah Dowdy is the founder and director of The Eagle's Nest Booking Agency in Nashville, Tennessee. I can sit for hours listening to her relay volumes of her own God Stories, and I'm honored to call her my friend.

❁ ❁ ❁

FOR YEARS, SARAH HAS BEEN fondly known as Bird Dog because of the way she searches out any given situation. She has headed up many ministries, each one passionately born out of a need that God had revealed to her.

The first of such ministries was called Damascus Road. It was initiated over twenty years ago by Sarah and three others who knew how to be Christians on Sunday, but wanted to know how to spill that knowledge over into the rest of the week.

They met in a small log cabin behind an old church to study God's Word and to get to know Him in a more intimate way. Specifically, they were petitioning the Lord that His wisdom, strength, and resurrection power would be unleashed in their everyday lives so that they could show young people how to do the same thing.

They moved four times within three years and ended up buying an old Bible college. Damascus Road grew to ten buildings on twenty acres of land and drew seven hundred kids a week for praise and worship and Bible study. Over the next ten years, thousands of kids came to know the Lord. Their annual overhead was one hundred thousand dollars and they prayed it in every year without solicitation.

Years later, Sarah learned that law enforcement officers in the area would drop juvenile offenders off at Damascus Road in hopes of getting help for them from God rather than sending them away to youth detention. Most of the time their efforts paid off.

Today many of those who once attended Damascus Road are in full-time ministry serving God throughout the world.

Guardian Angels is another ministry birthed out of a need that God revealed to Sarah. A couple of years ago, an elderly couple visiting Nashville from Spokane, Washington, were walking down the sidewalk when a gas leak caused a sewer cap to blow off. Severely burned, both were rushed in critical condition to the trauma center at Vanderbilt Hospital. Neither was expected to live.

After hearing this report, Sarah felt the Lord telling her to go to the hospital to minister to this couple's grown children. Because they were from out of town, they had no friends or family support in the area.

Sarah began to make daily trips to visit the family. As the couple's condition began to improve, Sarah found out that the one thing they'd wanted to do while they were in Nashville was to meet Barbara Mandrell. Sarah contacted Barbara and made arrangements for that to happen. Needless to say, the family was blown away. After months in the hospital and numerous surgeries, the couple were finally released from the hospital.

Because of this experience, others approached Sarah with the idea of helping others throughout the country who found themselves in similar crisis situations. She began establishing Guardian Angels chapters in other cities.

The most recent need came to her attention following a meeting that Sarah attended at her church. The River of Life Church has a Hispanic ministry that Sarah became acquainted with when she needed a translator for one of her Guardian Angels projects one Christmas.

Bande, one of the two women who heads up the Hispanic ministry, often works hand in hand with the Feed the Children organization to get food and clothing for people living in the projects. One day she received a call to bring an empty truck and come to the Feed the Children warehouse to pick up supplies. It had to be done immediately because they were getting in another shipment and needed to clear out space.

This particular day, Bande was caring for an elderly woman and that commitment presented a scheduling conflict. Bande asked if Sarah would be able to help by renting a truck and driving it to the Feed the Children warehouse to load up the supplies. Sarah quickly agreed, rented the truck, and headed for Feed the Children.

The truck was small and couldn't hold all they were offered on the first run, so Sarah made a second haul. By the time they had unloaded all the supplies, the hardware store where she had rented the truck had closed. She left the truck, unable to turn in the key or pay the tab.

She took the key by Bande's house and asked her if she would make sure the key was turned in by 11 A.M. the next morning so they wouldn't be charged for a second day. Bande agreed.

The next morning, Sarah got a call from Bande at 10:30 A.M. saying that she couldn't take the key back because she had just received the news that morning that her grandmother had passed away and she was en route to the airport.

Sarah knew she couldn't get there in time, but she headed to pick up the key and prayed that whoever was in charge at the hardware store would be merciful.

When Sarah arrived at the store, a woman attendant went out to check the mileage on the truck and commented on the extensive mileage and how costly the bill was going to be.

As Sarah began to explain to the woman how the church had used the truck, the woman seemed mesmerized. She told Sarah how she loved being involved with doing good deeds through her own church, but since her husband had become ill, she hadn't been able to participate. She only charged Sarah for a one-day rental and cut the fee for the mileage in half!

Sarah inquired about her husband's illness and learned that he was in his second round of leukemia. They were in the process of debating whether to try a bone marrow transplant from an unrelated donor that can sometimes have fatal complications.

Sarah began to share with the woman that she had been through an experience like that with a little boy through her Guardian Angels ministry.

One night the doctors told this boy's family that his body was rejecting the transplant and that apart from God intervening with a miracle, the boy would die within fifteen minutes. Sarah told the woman how she gathered with his family members and they pleaded that the blood of Jesus would come between what was good for him and what was bad for him. God performed a miracle and a year later the boy is alive, doing well.

The woman was encouraged by Sarah's story.

In the middle of a hardware store, with people checking out all around them, God sent a messenger in the form of Sarah "Bird Dog" Dowdy to bring hope to a woman who needed to be reminded of God's continual ability to perform miracles.

Because of her consistent desire to "bird dog" situations, Sarah has had the opportunity again and again to be privy to the inner workings of the One and True living God. She simply searches out what God is up to and joins Him!

❋ ❋ ❋

You will show me the path of life; In Your presence is fullness of joy; At Your right hand are pleasures forevermore.

PSALM 16:11

I THINK I LOVE MY WIFE

My friend Scott Wesley Brown has spent most of his adult life taking the message of Jesus Christ all around the globe through his music. He is a servant in the truest sense of the word and his stories are numerous. Here's one in his vast collection.

❀ ❀ ❀

WHILE ON A CAMPUS CRUSADE MISSION TRIP to Kenya for the purpose of showing the *Jesus* film, Christian artist Scott Wesley Brown had the opportunity to stay out among the Masai tribe. They are very beautiful people with a rich heritage.

The Masai tribe, however, is a primitive tribe and has lived the same way for thousands of years. They believe that God owns all the cows in the world, so the larger the herd, the more they are favored by God. Beginning at a very young age, the tribal fathers begin giving cows to their sons. The Masai also believe that when the sons reach manhood, they must go into the bush and kill a lion to prove that they are men. It is also prestigious to have many wives and children. These traditions have been passed down for generations.

A man's place in the Masai society, then, is measured by accomplishing these three things: killing a lion, receiving your herd of cows, and having many wives who bear many children.

Among all of the tribal people, women are thought of as property. They are bargained for and purchased just like cows, or as any other business transaction would be negotiated. A woman's purpose is to bear children, prepare meals, and keep the home clean while the husband tends to the cattle.

While in Kenya, Scott met a man named Jackson, who was born without a kneecap. He had a stick that he put underneath his arm at an angle to propel himself along. Because of his disability, Jackson had great difficulty in proving his manhood and establishing his significance in the village. There was no way he could herd cattle. There was no way for him to go up to Mount Kilimanjaro and slay a lion. The only thing that he could do was take as many wives and bear as many children as he possibly could.

After Jackson had taken his first wife, along came a missionary named John, who shared the gospel with him. As a result, Jackson received Jesus as his Savior and committed his life to the Lord.

Not immediately, but as he began to disciple Jackson, John informed him how God's word teaches husbands to love their wives. He told him that husbands must love their wives as Christ loves them. In a sense, they should be willing to lay down their lives for their wives.

This went against everything that Jackson had been taught. Men had no feelings at all toward women, other than to use them as a vehicle through which they fulfilled their manly status. A woman held no more status than a cow.

But Jackson really wanted to serve God.

He told John he would try to humble himself around his wife, but that he could never love her because she was his property. What the missionary was instructing him to do was like telling him to fall in love with his cow.

Then John informed Jackson that God's plan was that every man has only one wife—a shocking revelation.

John continued to disciple Jackson.

One day, John and Scott were walking through the bush and saw Jackson coming from the village, hobbling enthusiastically toward them. When Jackson had reached them, he said, "John, I have an announcement to make." This was a rather formal statement for Jackson.

John stopped and responded, "What is it, Jackson?"

In a quiet voice, Jackson whispered, "Don't tell anyone, but I think I love my wife."

Jackson wanted to please God so much that God changed his heart and allowed him to fall in love with his wife.

On the airplane ride back to the states, Scott thought about America, our divorce rate, and the way we throw our marriages away like Dixie cups. Seeing the power of God move in Jackson's life made Scott grateful for his wife and for the gift of easily being able to love her.

In the years since, when Scott and his wife have experienced difficulties in their relationship, Scott pictures Kenya and a villager named Jackson hobbling up to him and proclaiming, "John, I think I love my wife."

❀ ❀ ❀

Because he has set his love upon Me, therefore I will deliver him. I will set him on high, because he has known My name. He shall call upon Me, and I will answer him; I will be with him in trouble; I will deliver him and honor him. With long life I will satisfy him, and show him My salvation.

PSALM 91:14–16

99

Mama's Been Talkin' to Jesus Again!

Aaron Tippin's first country nightclub performance in 1990 resulted in a record deal with RCA. A string of multi-million-selling albums and concert dates with superstars such as Brooks and Dunn, Reba McEntire, and Hank Williams Jr. has made him one of the most successful country acts today.

I interviewed Aaron from his cell phone as he was driving down the highway. I could hear kids chattering in the background, a country radio station humming on the radio, and the sound of wind whistling through the car. It was a perfectly staged setting to interview a true country artist.

As a young boy raised in the mountains of South Carolina, Aaron Tippin broke out of the rock band trends that his peers were hooked on and became wildly passionate about traditional country music. He began performing in local honky-tonks in the 1970s and when his teenage marriage ended, he decided to pursue his dream of making a living at writing, playing, and singing his music.

In the early eighties, Aaron squeaked out a living working the nightshift at an aluminum rolling mill in Kentucky and commuted to Nashville's Music Row every day to write songs.

In 1986, he competed on The Nashville Network's talent contest, *You Can Be a Star*, and landed a publishing contract for songwriting.

About that same time, Aaron took up competitive weight lifting and faithfully trained every afternoon, building his frame to a forty-seven-inch chest and sixteen-inch biceps. It was a way to stay in shape and it created the potential for extra income when he entered competitions.

His twenty-four-hour schedule was rigorously packed with activity. For months on end, he worked the midnight shift at the factory, commuted to Nashville to write music, did his late afternoon workout, drove back to Kentucky, took in a few hours of sleep, and awakened to perform the same routine, day after day.

Every other weekend Aaron had custody of his baby daughter, and he would drive home to South Carolina to spend it with her. While there, Aaron's mother would inquire about how things were going in Nashville and his reply would always be the same: "Oh everything's great, mama! Things are going really well!"

Aaron remembers one weekend in particular when he was really having a rough time. He was tired, frustrated, and discouraged. It was 6:00 A.M. and as he ended his midnight shift, he threw his empty lunch pail into his truck and headed to South Carolina for the weekend.

Aaron was exhausted from the schedule he was keeping and wondered if all of his hard work was ever going to pay off. For years, he had dreamed of having a recording contract and even with all of the exposure as a songwriter, he had yet to get recognition as an artist. Until he was able to write his songs *and* sing, he didn't feel he'd be able to make enough income to quit his job at the mill.

For the entire drive to South Carolina, Aaron prayed about whether he should throw in the towel or continue hanging in there. That weekend, when his mom asked him how things were going, once again he lied and told her all was well!

After the weekend was over, Aaron packed up his truck and left South Carolina, heading back to Nashville for a morning full of writing appointments. As usual, his mom had put a snack of some kind in his lunch pail so he would have something to eat as he drove.

As Aaron opened his lunch pail, he found something neatly tucked underneath his snack. It was a book entitled *The Power of Positive Thinking,* by Norman Vincent Peale.

Aaron smiled and cried simultaneously while considering, "But how in the world did Mama know that I was having such a tough time, and even more so than usual?"

The answer came quickly: "Mama's been talkin' to Jesus again!"

Aaron immediately began thanking God for a mom who prays over every issue of life. And for a mom who not only heard from God, but passed along what she thought God instructed her to do by giving Aaron the encouragement he so desperately needed."

When Aaron arrived for his writing appointment in Nashville, he and his co-writing partner for the day, Jerry Salley, wrote a song called "Mama's Been Talkin' to Jesus Again."

"Later that night on my ride home to Kentucky, I received a great revelation from God on several fronts," Aaron recalled. "I realized that I needed to stop trying to do everything on my own. I also realized that if God created the universe and everything in it, He could provide for all of my career goals, if that was God's plan for my life.

"I also realized that what I had thought were my private secrets weren't really secrets at all. I began to see that it was prideful to try and cover up that I was going through hard times. I knew that nothing could be hidden from God and that *almost* nothing could be hidden from my mom!

"I began to cast all of my cares upon the Lord, instead of continuing to try and handle everything myself. I also began spending more time with the Lord . . . so much so that I soon felt like Jesus had become my best friend. God used my hard times to develop my dependence on Him."

Aaron saw his dedication beginning to pay off when he started winning barbell competitions. Even better, his success as a songwriter flourished when Charley Pride, David Ball, The Kingsman, The Mid-South Boys, Mark Collie, and many others recorded his songs.

Finally in 1990, Aaron's dream to become a recording artist finally came true. While performing his first Nashville show, RCA Records offered him a recording contract. Since that time, his albums have sold millions and he has performed with country superstars such as Reba McEntire, Brooks and Dunn, and Hank Williams Jr. His latest release on the Lyric Street label, *What This Country Needs,* is a smash hit.

Aaron manages to enjoy every second of his successful career. Not a day passes that he doesn't reflect back on his meager beginnings, thanking God for His faithfulness and for a mom that prayed for him then and continues to pray for him now.

Each time all of the past memories of Aaron's extremely successful career rise up in his spirit and reel through his mind, a prominent picture forms that he knows will always remain. It's of a woman wearing an apron, waving from the front porch as he drives away in his truck. As she smiles, waves, and blows kisses, there's one thing he knew for certain then and continues to be grateful for now: Mama's been talkin' to Jesus again.

❀ ❀ ❀

When my heart is overwhelmed; lead me to a rock that is higher than I.

PSALM 61:2

103

LEARNING TO TRUST

"Howard Hewitt," one *Rolling Stone* writer claims, "is the premier vocalist in the post-Marvin Gaye era of romantic pop."

Formerly the lead singer for the award-winning group Shalimar, he's responsible for selling over ten million records worldwide. In the mid-eighties, his solo career took off when his first single rocketed to #1 on the Billboard charts. A series of hits followed: "Stay," "I Commit to Love," "Strange Relationship," "Once, Twice, Three Times," and "Show Me." His song "Say Amen" has become a gospel classic. His recorded duets with Anita Baker, Dionne Warwick, Brenda Russell, and Stacy Lattisaw have won critical accolades. Producer/artist/songwriter Babyface says, "Of all the singers working today, Howard Hewitt is among the finest."

My friend Zoro, the drummer, put me in contact with Howard. One of my favorite memories of Howard is during his appearance on *The Arsenio Hall Show*.

Arsenio asked, "Howard, I understand that you pray about *everything* . . . what songs to sing, what gigs to take, how to invest your money . . . everything."

"That's right," Howard responded very matter-of-factly.

"And you say that you actually hear the voice of God giving you answers?" Arsenio inquired.

"Absolutely," Howard said without reservation.

"Well, I get down on my knees and pray to God all the time and I never hear Him say anything back to me," Arsenio replied.

Without missing a beat Howard said, "Well, maybe you need to stay down a little longer!"

Of course everyone, including Arsenio, got a big laugh out of Howard's response.

I enjoyed getting to meet Howard by phone, recount his interview on *Arsenio*, and thank him for his boldness.

❀ ❀ ❀

FROM THE TIME HE WAS TEN YEARS OLD, Howard Hewitt sang gospel music in church. His church didn't have a regular choir, rather a finely tuned and vocally precisioned group of singers. Singing in this group dug roots deep into Howard's young heart and cultivated his love for rhythm and harmony.

Howard's group performed along with some of the top gospel groups in the country, putting on shows through a professional gospel promoter in and around Cleveland, Ohio.

In 1976, Howard moved to Los Angeles, formed another group, and in 1977 began touring with them overseas. They performed there for about eight months, came home for a month, and then returned for another eight months.

During the month that Howard was home, he met a girl and they began dating. When he returned to Europe, they stayed in contact and when he came back to the States, they ended up moving in together.

About two months later, his girlfriend informed him that they were expecting a child. Having just recently returned from Europe, Howard only had about five hundred dollars to his name. He was just starting to investigate work opportunities and was completely thrown off guard with the announcement of his impending fatherhood. She wanted to keep the baby. But his first response was, "Whoa, baby! Don't you think we should get a second opinion?"

Howard recalls, "It was a very confusing time in my life. I was young and had dreams to pursue with my music. Now I was faced with the reality, as well as the responsibility and consequences of my actions."

Then Howard remembered something his mom had said to him: "When you feel your life is surrounded on all sides, the only place to look is up."

So, Howard went to visit Crenshaw Christian Church, pastored by a man named Fred Price. When he heard the sermon that day, he felt as though Pastor Price knew everything about him and was reading his "heart-letter."

At the end of the sermon, the pastor gave an invitation. He invited those who had never accepted Jesus as their personal Savior to come to the altar. He also invited those who had prayer requests. He then invited those who had slipped away from their walk with God and needed assurance of their salvation and of God's love for them.

"I knew that invitation was for me. I quickly moved forward to the front of the church. One of the volunteers ushered me off to a private area on the side and began to pray with me."

Using the scriptures, the volunteer showed Howard that he was a child of God and reassured him of his position in Christ.

"I left the church floating on a cloud. God had given me confidence and direction for what I must do. Even though it made me cringe, I knew that I must look for a nine-to-five job so that I could begin preparing for the birth of my baby."

The next day, Howard got up, dressed in a suit, and hit the street in search of a job. By the end of the day, he'd been hired to work in a clothing store. Howard praised the Lord for His provision and faithfulness!

"I began to spend a good deal of time reading my Bible and praying. I had an insatiable desire to grow in knowledge of the Lord and apply God's ways to my daily life. I wanted to establish a relationship with God and to really *know* Him, not just facts about Him. I knew it would take time to develop the relationship, but my desire was to have God as my best friend."

Three weeks after getting his new job, Howard got a call from a friend named Tammy Gibson, who used to sing background vocals for Stevie Wonder. Tammy asked Howard if he could do a background session for a man named Jeff Bowen over at Motown. Jeff was putting together a new group and an album for Eddie Hazel, who had played guitar for the Funkadelics.

Jeff offered Howard a position in the group.

Howard also joined AFTRA (a singers' union) and began making ninety dollars an hour every day. Since everything was turning around for him financially, he was able to quit his job at the clothing store. His girlfriend's pregnancy was also going well.

After a time, the singing job began to get a little shaky, so Howard was delighted when he received a call from Jeffrey Day from the group, Shalimar. Jeffrey had met Howard when he was rehearsing his group to go overseas. Jeff explained to Howard that Shalimar was on a promotional tour in New York and that after a disagreement, their lead singer had walked out on them. He offered Howard an equal position in the group and wanted him to join them as their lead singer.

It just so happened that Shalimar's record company was located down on the ninth floor of the building in which Howard was sitting. Jeffrey told him to go downstairs, where his contracts would be drawn up and waiting on him for his review.

Howard went down to the ninth floor and met with the powers that be, including Dick Griffey. The deal was explained to him, but Howard needed to tie up some loose ends with his current job. However, he would definitely be interested in joining Shalimar.

The next morning, Howard went to Dick Griffey's house to view one of Shalimar's videos. Dick had never heard Howard sing so he asked him to belt out a few bars.

Howard said, "Okay Lord, it's You and me," and he began to sing. After one verse and a chorus, Dick excused himself and went upstairs to get some cash for Howard. He wanted to make sure that Howard would be able to leave money for his wife and still have enough for the road. He handed Howard an airline ticket on the red-eye for New York.

Howard had rehearsals on Sunday and did his first television show with Shalimar on Monday.

"Only a short time before, I had been expecting a baby and working in a clothing store. I thought my dreams of making a living through music had been dashed, but God had other plans. I found out that I could become a daddy and fulfill my dreams at the same time. God had it all under control, as I was faithfully trying to learn to trust my new best friend."

Those who trust in the LORD are as Mount Zion, unmoved by any circumstance.

PSALM 125:1, THE LIFE APPLICATION BIBLE

JEHOVAH JIREH

Tiffany signed her first major recording contract with MCA Records at the age of fifteen. Her first single, "I Think We're Alone Now," stayed on the Billboard charts for thirteen weeks and her album, *Tiffany*, went to #1.

Not only has she had numerous #1 singles and albums that have sold multi-platinum, she also had three songs on the soundtrack to the animated film, *The Jetsons*, where she was cast as the voice of Judy Jetson.

I met Tiffany through her former bodyguard Frank D'Amato. We spoke by phone from her studio where she was working on a new record.

FROM AS YOUNG AS TWO YEARS OLD, Tiffany can remember wanting to be a singer. Reading the list of her impressive career credits, you'd assume that she would have to be middle-aged to have accomplished all that she has. But her first record was released when she was only sixteen.

By twenty, she was mature beyond her years and desired to come off the road. Although she was young, she wanted to experience marriage and motherhood. These goals became a priority to her.

She began to pray that God would send her a Christian life partner. Tiffany met all types of nice guys, but no one that she felt was really "the one."

Tiffany recalls, "One of my bodyguards, Frank, suggested to

me that I be more specific in my prayers. I took his advice and later, a young makeup artist named Bulmaro came along. Within a very short time, we knew we were meant for each other.

"As we exited the church on our wedding day, there was a rainbow arched across the sky. I thought about how God used the rainbow to signify that He always keeps His promises. I thought about the fact that Bulmaro and our marriage to each other was God fulfilling His promise to me. I felt that the rainbow was a personal reminder: "Trust in Him and He shall give you the desires of your heart." (Psalm 37:3–4)

"When Bulmaro and I had our first baby, I noticed something amazing as we were leaving the hospital—a double rainbow across the horizon. *Another* gentle reminder from God that He had fulfilled both of my heart's desires . . . to be a wife and now a mother!"

Because of her schedule, Tiffany had never been afforded the luxury of enjoying a personal life. She decided to take a well-deserved hiatus to enjoy her new son. It was an interlude she'd never forget.

She didn't worry about her career. She had always felt that whenever she decided to go back, she could simply pick up where she had left off and do what she had done in the past—sing.

In the spring of 1994 and Tiffany was about to return to work. She and her band were booked to begin shows at the Hilton in Las Vegas.

Since it had only been two years since she had been actively recording and touring, it came as a surprise to Tiffany that she had to basically start over again in establishing her name recognition. The salary she was offered was not nearly what she had made in the past. Moreover, it cost a lot of money to assemble and rehearse a band and put a live show together.

She also experienced some security problems at the hotel. Overzealous fans caused her to have to hire a bodyguard. Consequently, most of what she was being paid went toward expenses. She was willing to make the sacrifice, however, to rekindle public interest so that she could continue doing what she'd always had such a passion to do.

Although being a makeup artist is usually a lucrative profession, Bulmaro wasn't bringing in any money either because he was on the road with Tiffany. The financial burdens were becoming increasingly stressful to the couple. Just keeping the show going in Las Vegas was hard enough, but they also had to keep up their home in California.

"We knew that in an emergency, we could borrow money from our parents, but we elected not to go that route. We also knew we could ask the hotel management for an advance, but being a private person, I didn't feel that was a good option for us."

Tiffany and her group were doing three shows a night. The never-ending pace and the financial pressure were keeping her exhausted. One week, things got particularly stressful because of little extras like dry cleaning and the bill for security. That's when the heartbreaking reality really hit. The ship was sinking.

Tiffany and her husband knelt in their room praying for God to supernaturally intervene and send them a breakthrough. If a miracle didn't occur, they were going to have to cancel their engagement at the Hilton. They couldn't afford to work this hard and continue losing money, but they were determined to stay positive and allow God to teach them something powerful, even in the midst of their difficulty.

"We asked God to somehow provide for us until the next payday and then to give us wisdom to re-evaluate our situation so we would know what to do. We said, God, You say that You'll supply all our needs according to Your riches in glory through Christ Jesus. We're asking You to be true to Your word.

They said their final amen and went downstairs to have dinner with their last fifty dollars until the next payday.

As they were finishing their meal and standing to leave, an older gentleman approached the table.

"What a beautiful baby," he said with a smile.

"Thank you," they responded.

The man slipped something into Tiffany's hand. As he turned to walk away, he said, "I think the baby needs this."

As his words reached Tiffany's ears, she looked down to see what was in her hand. It was a hundred-dollar bill. Her mouth dropped and she quickly looked up to find the man. Her intention was to thank him, but to decline the money. He was nowhere to be found.

Tiffany began to cry as she realized that this man's gift was an answer to their prayer. God—Jehovah Jireh, our Provider—had provided until the next payday. Tiffany's faith was strengthened. God had always provided for her in the past and He had done it again.

Be anxious for nothing but in everything by prayer and supplication with thanksgiving let your requests be made known to God and the peace of God, which passes all understanding, will guard your hearts and minds through Christ Jesus.

PHILIPPIANS 4:6–7

BILLBOARDS

An award-winning producer, writer, director, radio personality, and scholar, Dr. Ted Baehr is the Chairman of the Christian Film and Television Commission, a non-profit organization committed to educating the entertainment industry and the general public on the media's impact on its audiences. He also serves as the publisher for *Movieguide*, a family guide to entertainment, and hosts a syndicated radio and television program by the same name.

I met Ted when I attended an awards banquet hosted by his organization to honor excellence in film and television. The work that Ted does is extremely important and his involvement with Hollywood studios and his strides to educate the public on the effects of media in our society has served us all well.

❀ ❀ ❀

IN LATIN, THE WORD MIRACLE can also mean billboards—little signs or reminders, so to speak. In his travels around the world, Dr. Ted Baehr and his crew have experienced a myriad of billboards.

On one trip, Dr. Baehr and his crew arrived in Jerusalem to shoot a documentary. As it turned out, the host church that was supposed to be responsible for making all the production arrangements had dropped the ball. Upset by all of the confusion, and needing to find a moment of solace, the director of the show, Tom, whose child was terminally ill in the States, decided to go into the Church of the Nativity. He went there to pray that God

113

would straighten things out, let him complete his work on the documentary and return to Israel with his wife within the year so she could experience the Holy Land firsthand.

Unfortunately the mishap with all of the production arrangements was not resolved. Thankfully, Jerusalem Capitol Studios, which now serves as a studio for TBN, intervened and eventually, bailed them out, and they were able to complete their project. Even with all the challenges along the way, before leaving to return home, Tom told God that he'd like to come back to Jerusalem in a year or so and bring his wife with him.

Shortly after returning home, Tom's three-year-old daughter died. After a time of grieving, and in an attempt to get back to his work, Tom met Ted in New York to do post-production on another project. While in the studio, Tom got a call from the State of Israel inviting him to come back to the country. It had been just about a year since he had been there.

Ted said to Tom, "Well, you got your answer to prayer. You asked God to let you go back in a year and here's your invitation." Tom's wife was able to go too, just has Tom had hoped.

Meanwhile, Ted found himself experiencing some envious thoughts about Tom and his wife getting to go to Israel. He, too, was feeling led to go back overseas, so he began telling God how he wished he could travel around the world again.

After arriving at home, Ted's assistant informed him that a man in North Carolina had been frantically trying to reach him. He wanted to send Ted around the world to do a documentary. At the last minute, one of the cameramen scheduled to go on the shoot had to cancel due to an illness in his family. Although it had been years before, Ted's partner, Sam, had once been a cameraman. The vacant slot enabled Sam to become part of the team, along with Ted.

They went to Sri Lanka, and while there, Ted and Sam used a state-of-the-art JVC high-powered camera, hot off the presses from Japan. No one anywhere had a camera like this one.

At one point, a chip went out, crippling the shoot.

There they were, in the deepest part of Sri Lanka. Several of the Arabs with whom they were working claimed they knew where to get the chip. Ted and Sam were both thinking the same thing: "Yeah, right." "Follow us," they insisted.

Reluctantly, Ted and Sam followed their guides for hours through unknown territory out in the middle of the jungle with a war in full bloom. They finally arrived at a small hut-like stall, where a small, thin Arab man greeted them. The guides explained what they needed and the man went to the back part of his dwelling. He returned with a glass jar containing the chip they needed.

"Unbelievable!" Ted recalls, "We were in a remote, desolate area of the world! Who but God could have orchestrated this?"

Soon after finding the chip, the project was completed.

On another production trip, Ted had to leave South Africa in order to return to the states for a scheduled television appearance. In his baggage, he carried the film that he needed for his interview.

"When I arrived in London, I was informed there was a suspected bomb threat. Not only did I miss my flight, but they didn't know where my bags were. I insisted on keeping my commitment for the interview and would try an alternative route to get home."

Upon landing at LAX in the middle of the night, Ted began to search for his bags. None of the three airlines on which he had traveled had seen them; therefore, Ted asked God to help him find his bags so he would have the film he needed for his interview. And as Ted looked around in the deserted terminal, there were his bags, tagged with beautiful, bright orange South African security clearance tape. It was one of the most beautiful sights Ted had ever seen!

As Ted puts it, "God cares about every detail of our lives and delights in giving us the desires of our hearts. He even supplies all the billboards along the way just to remind us!"

❁ ❁ ❁

Blessed be the Lord, who daily loads us with benefits.

PSALM 68:19

No Wonder

I T WAS AFTER 3 A.M. and I had to catch a 7 A.M. flight to Los Angeles. Like any good workaholic, I had scheduled fourteen meetings over the next three days. Anyone else would have realized the insanity of setting up such an itinerary.

My insane schedule was not my only point of dread. Over the previous few weeks, I had encountered much discouragement in preparation for this trip. The reality that there was a chance I'd never be able to actually make a living as a writer/producer was staring me in the face.

Five years earlier, I had left the stability of a nine-to-five job as a dental hygienist. The fact that I had even pursued a profession that required me to be up, showered, dressed, and able to construct full sentences by 8 A.M. while gazing, with some semblance of interest, into the mouth of a total stranger, was still a mystery to me. What had I been thinking? At least the paycheck I was receiving had allowed me the luxury of the lifestyle to which I had become accustomed—living indoors.

I was grateful to be writing songs—something for which I had unquenchable thirst. My ambitions were grand. I wanted to do everything.

Still, the transition was tough.

I had spent five years having no idea just how God would provide for my financial needs every month. Yet, He had never let me down. I'd really learned a thing or two about scrimping, trusting, and faith. There was certainly nothing wrong that.

In the beginning, my heart's desire was to write songs, books, screenplays, music videos, television shows, and films. Many were concerned that I was expecting too much. They felt that my dreams

116

and goals were too spread out. In fact, one day while lunching at the Buckhead Diner, my friend and music attorney, James Randolph Smith, confronted me with an important question.

"If you could do only one thing, what would it be?" he asked.

"Well, I couldn't do just one thing," I answered. "Why would I want to? I would get bored."

"Hypothetically," he persisted.

"I can't think about something that's never going to happen," I insisted.

He said he would ask me again in about five years.

Well, here I was, five years later, asking myself the same question.

I was beginning to wonder if I had misread God in leaving such a dependable job behind. I had developed several projects during my new adventure and had even signed a coproduction deal for a children's television series with one of my heroes of all time, Dick Clark. But nothing had been placed for airing, so I was technically still not on the map. A promising career is not the same as a successful career.

I was getting tired of rejection. I also longed to get paid for my efforts. Time and time again, I had evaluated my work against those who had "made it" and I knew that I was just as talented as any of them were. So, I wondered, why all the waiting? Why all the delays?

On this trip to Los Angeles, most of the meetings I had scheduled were regarding television and film projects. But in my sleep-deprived stupor, the night before leaving, I had suddenly decided to take a few of my songs on tape, along with lyric sheets, just in case I had a chance to pitch a song along the way. It was late one evening and I was really getting punchy. All I had left to do before I could sleep was to print out my lyric sheets. So I pulled them up on the computer screen and hit "print."

As I waited for the lyrics to print, I began to pray. I told God that I was tired and discouraged. I told Him I had tried with all my might to pursue this new career. I told Him how I longed for the day when I could experience the harvest of my efforts. I had planted so many seeds. I had watered, weeded, fertilized, and pruned. When was it going to be my turn?

I told God that I had seen His faithfulness all around me, and that I knew He was able to do anything. I continued by saying that I was just *wondering* if it would ever happen in my life, personally? I was *wondering* if I would ever see the fruits of my labor?

I was just *wondering*.

Just then, my printer jammed. It spit out a sheet of paper with only one line of my song printed on it. The line that printed was the third line of the second verse. No title, no author, no first verse, no first chorus, no first two lines or last line of the second verse, no second chorus and no publishing information. There was just one lone line on the paper. The line read: "There's no need for you to have to wonder."

I looked at the page again. It was so obvious. I laughed and cried simultaneously. I was thrilled at the way the God of the universe had just specifically answered my question. I neatly folded that sheet of paper and put it in my Bible so it could be with me always.

After a little more than two hours of sleep, I bolted out of bed the next morning as though I had been on a six-month sabbatical. I was energized, refreshed, and renewed.

And I was certain of one thing: *There's no need for me to have to wonder.*

❀ ❀ ❀

I will bless the LORD who has given me counsel; my heart also instructs me in the night seasons. I have set the LORD always before me; because He is at my right hand I shall not be moved.

PSALM 16:7–8

ENTERTAINING ANGELS

Matt King's Atlantic Records debut album, *Five O'Clock Hero*, saw great success. His second album, *Hard Country*, is climbing the charts, and I predict many #1 singles off this record. Matt is also a highly sought-after songwriter. He collects guitars and knives and enjoys reading Irish literature and Indian lore.

Matt and I began his interview as he was going to a meeting and we completed it by phone from his home later that evening. After the interview, we chatted for a while and he played me his first single off of *Hard Country* over the phone. It sounded like a hit to me!

Matt and I have now become email pals. One of the most interesting things about him is that he seems to be in tune with the world around him. I think that's why he's become privy to certain heavenly events.

🏵 🏵 🏵

MAKING IT IN THE MUSIC BUSINESS can be quite a challenge. When first arriving in Nashville, every dreamer assumes it will be just a matter of seconds, minutes, or days until he or she is discovered. When weeks turn to months and months turn to years, doubt sets in and enthusiasm dwindles.

Yet, for anyone who has ever had that dream, the glimmer of possibility never seems to let go of one's heart. Time and time again, there are stories told about an artist who was close to packing up and moving back to Somewhere, USA, when BOOM—the call comes and a deal is made.

Matt King is one such story. A gifted singer and songwriter, he went to Nashville with big dreams and high hopes.

After he got to Nashville, he did all the right things. He dropped off cassette tapes demonstrating his vocal abilities at all the record companies. He sang at writers' nights, so that people could hear him sing his songs and play his guitar. He tacked his name on studio bulletin boards, offering his services to sing or play guitar on other artists' records. He passed out business cards to publishers, trying to play or sing on studio demo sessions while working hard to develop relationships within the industry.

And while he did everything he could to squeak out a living while pursuing a record deal for himself, but it was beginning to look like a deal would never come.

Matt had gone through all of his savings and was only weeks away from having to declare bankruptcy.

That's when the phone rang.

It was the President and Head of Marketing and A&R at Atlantic Records, informing him that they wanted to sign him as an artist. Matt's dreams were being realized and he was being given the opportunity to cut a record.

Negotiating the record contract was a long and drawn out process, but Matt's deal was finally signed. Along with the signing came a six-figure publishing deal.

The first thing he did was go to Taco Bell and order one of everything. As he exited the restaurant carrying his huge sack of food, he noticed a homeless man across the way.

He had seen this man before, so Matt got into his car and drove to where the man was sitting. As Matt approached the man, Matt rolled down his car window, spoke to him, and then handed him the sack full of food.

"God bless you," the man said, appreciatively.

Matt returned the salutation and drove away.

Some months later, Matt was in a coffee shop and this same man walked in. Matt invited him to have a coffee with him and asked the man his name.

"Paul," he said.

Matt began asking Paul about himself. Paul was a drug addict. As he talked, Matt noticed that several of Paul's fingers were severely bent, probably from arthritis. Paul told Matt about how a car had hit him twice. Matt quickly realized that Paul was a lot younger than he looked. He was in bad shape and street life had really taken its toll on him.

Matt had also noticed that every time he had seen Paul walking the streets, he always carried a folder with him.

"What's in the folder?" Matt inquired.

"They're pictures of Jesus," Paul replied.

"Wow, can I see them?" Matt asked.

Paul opened up the folder. Some were pen and ink, others crayon. Paul had drawn every one of the renderings and they were magnificent! The beauty of this man's art stunned Matt. He handed Paul a twenty-dollar bill as a gift and they continued talking.

"What made you decide to start drawing pictures of Jesus?" Matt asked.

"One time, when I was on an LSD trip and close to dying, Jesus came to me. I saw Him as clearly as I'm looking at you now. Ever since that day, I've not been able to stop drawing Him."

As Matt left Paul that day, he thanked God for prompting him to take the time to sit and talk with Paul. Matt realized that in giving to this precious street person, it was he, not Paul, who had been blessed.

Matt has now made it his mission to notice others in need. Since that time, he has had many other similar experiences because of his openness to be used by God to reach out to those less fortunate. It was Matt's waiting period between arriving in Nashville and signing his record deal that helped groom him to be perceptive to the needs of others.

Matt King learned that when we give out of a heart of gratitude, what we get in return will far exceed our gesture.

God said it best:

DONNA I. DOUGLAS

❀ ❀ ❀

Do not forget to entertain strangers, for by so doing some have unwittingly entertained angels.

HEBREWS 13:2

A WALKING MIRACLE

Among many other titles, Tayo Reed is a former cheerleader for the Atlanta Falcons, dancer for the Atlanta Hawks, represented Coca Cola in the 1996 Olympics, and was a Nitro girl with World Championship Wrestling.

I met Tayo through our mutual friend, voice instructor Vicki Gray. She told her story to me one of the first times we met and it serves as a great encouragement to anyone facing challenges in their life.

I N THE SPRING OF 1970, in Birmingham, Alabama, a fourteen-year-old drug addict gave birth to a beautiful baby girl. For as long as she can remember, Tayo Reed was tossed around between the homes of various relatives, neighbors, and friends, never knowing where her next meal would come from or where she would sleep at night. This type of instability continued throughout her childhood.

As a young girl, she found great pride in putting on shows for the other children in the neighborhood. Dancing, singing, and acting were the three loves of her young life. Her talents became her friends because they could be taken along with her no matter where she was sent to live. It was through entertaining others and hearing their applause that she felt a sense of accomplishment and self-worth. She also learned that she could make friends by teaching others how to do what she did.

When Tayo moved to the Atlanta area to live with a relative, she investigated her options for higher learning and applied for a scholarship to The School of the Performing Arts in Atlanta, Georgia. Through her own initiative, she was accepted. Tayo excelled throughout her high school years and graduated when she was eighteen.

It was her love of dancing, singing, and acting that kept her off the streets, and she was determined to pursue her dream of a career in the entertainment industry. Immediately following her graduation, she began auditioning for the many opportunities that seemed to be coming her way.

Then it happened.

The godfather of soul, Mr. James Brown, hired Tayo as one of his background singers. Following that, R&B star Pebbles recognized her special talents and hired Tayo to choreograph her world tour.

Even as she was beginning to experience great success, however, there was something missing her life—something she was constantly working to resolve. Because Tayo didn't want her five-year-old brother, Charles, to experience the horrendous childhood she had, Tayo had saved every penny she made in hopes that she could prove to the courts that she was capable of taking over custody of him.

Tayo recalls, "Just prior to my nineteenth birthday, Charles and I were reunited. We shared bunk beds in a one-bedroom apartment. It may not have seemed like much to other people, but to us, it was just fine because we were finally back together."

Next, Tayo became a Falcons cheerleader and then a dancer for the Atlanta Hawks. Both of these jobs gave her the chance to use her dancing talent and to do many public appearances where she could meet and influence young fans.

Tayo then auditioned to be a background singer/dancer, and not just a choreographer, for Pebbles. She was hired, and touring with Pebbles in this capacity served as another great opportunity.

After her stint with Pebbles ended, Tayo spent fifty to sixty hours a week working three to four jobs just to make ends meet. She started a dance school, not only as a source of income, but to offer an after-school alternative to inner city kids. She enjoyed the opportunity to make a difference in the lives of children by building their self-esteem and encouraging them.

Tayo tells what happened to her after the 1996 Olympics: "I returned to a hectic work schedule. One night while driving home from an appointment, I fell asleep at the wheel and drove my car underneath a semitruck. Upon impact, and only because I was asleep, I fell to the right and across the seat. The impact sheared off the roof of my car. When the emergency team arrived, they were astonished that I had not been killed."

Not long after her accident, she got a call that would change her life again—an opportunity to audition to be a Nitro Girl for World Championship Wrestling. She got the job. Tayo would continue teaching at her dance studio, but God had provided a job with a salary substantial enough so she could resign all of her other jobs.

As a Nitro girl, Tayo did many extensive personal appearances and had numerous opportunities to share how her faith in God had kept her on the high road during difficult times.

Tayo is longer a Nitro girl, but she continues to speak at youth events, where she shares the importance of staying in school, staying off of drugs and practicing abstinence. Tayo is currently pursuing her latest dream to become a country singer.

Statistically, Tayo should have followed in the footsteps of her mother— promiscuity, drugs, dropout, and welfare recipient. Instead, she chose to believe what God has to say about her. She feels that "no matter where we come from or how life starts out, there is a loving God who has promised to never leave us or forsake us. He also has a plan and a purpose for every life.

"I'm an example of an individual whose trust rests in God," says Tayo. "No matter what any of us faces in life, God is bigger than our problems and is capable of resolving any challenges we encounter along the way. Empowered by Him, we can all become walking miracles."

❀ ❀ ❀

For You formed my inward parts; You covered me in my mother's womb. I will praise You, for I am fearfully and wonderfully made; marvelous are Your works, and that my soul knows very well. How precious also are Your thoughts to me, O God! How great is the sum of them! If I should count them, they would be more in number than the sand.

PSALM 139:13–14, 17–18

126

A Match Made in Heaven

Fred and Wanda Collins served as house parents at the Clay Home for Unwed Mother's until the church that owned the facility decided to close its doors. It was during their tenure that I had the privilege of getting to know them and their daughters, Candice and Courtney.

I interviewed Wanda while she was back in the Atlanta area for a Clay Home reunion.

❀ ❀ ❀

WHILE SERVING AT THE CLAY HOME, Fred and Wanda experienced miracles on a daily basis. They witnessed what love, compassion, and sharing knowledge could do to transform lives. Along with an excellent staff and a host of eager volunteers, they helped equip women in crisis pregnancies with the physical, mental, emotional, and spiritual tools needed to accept the responsibility of motherhood. Wanda and Fred always treated each resident as though they were family.

One night, Fred began suffering terrible pain in his back and chest. Convinced that it was a heart attack, Wanda called 911. The emergency crew determined that it wasn't his heart, but that the pain was most likely caused by kidney stones.

Fred saw his physician the following day. X-rays were taken, kidney stones were confirmed, and he was given medication to dissolve them.

The X-rays that were taken also detected a problem in Fred's lungs. Additional testing revealed that he was experiencing a recurrence of melanoma. The prognosis was terminal and Fred was only given a few months to live. Being only forty-two and looking forward to a long and productive life, Fred and Wanda were devastated.

During Fred's illness, family and friends flocked in from all over the country to visit him. One couple, Hal and Kathy Posner, came on numerous occasions to help around the home. The Collins and the Posners had met years back while attending the same church in Savannah. The friendship continued when Fred and Wanda moved to the Clay Home and Hal and Kathy made weekend trips to help with painting, assist in maintaining the grounds, and collect baby furniture, clothes, and food for the girls.

Upon hearing the news of Fred's illness, Hal and Kathy immediately called their long-time friends and prayer partners, Dr. Rick and Jan Thomas, who lived in Ohio. Hal asked them to keep Fred and Wanda in their prayers, and Rick and Jan committed to do just that.

Following numerous traditional and alternative treatments, Fred lost his battle with cancer. Wanda made the decision that she and the girls would stay at the Clay Home to continue the ministry, but two months after Fred's death, the Clay Home was closed.

So Wanda decided to return to Savannah. For the first few months, they lived with her brother and his wife. Just five weeks before Fred passed away, her brother's eight-year-old daughter had died from spinal meningitis and Wanda and her brother decided they could help each other work through their grief.

Wanda explains, "After a time, I decided that my girls and I needed our own place, so for a short time we moved into a small house next to our church. The location was a good one because the girls were involved in a lot of youth activities and could walk across the parking lot to participate."

Later, Wanda accepted a position at a new home for unwed

mothers in Savannah called The Living Vine. She and her girls moved in, along with Joanie Perry, a social worker who had worked with them at the Clay Home. The girls were thrilled because life had been too quiet living in homes with less than fifteen other people.

Meanwhile, Wanda's friend Hal Posner received the devastating news that his close friend and prayer partner, Dr. Rick, had suddenly lost his wife, Jan, due to an embolism. When Rick and Jan married, she had three-year-old twins, Laura and Dana, whom Rick had adopted. Together, they had three more girls, Jenette, and another set of twins, Erica and Liz. Thus, when Jan died, Rick was left with five daughters.

Rick was distraught. Jan had been homeschooling the girls and had run their home with efficiency that he could not begin to accomplish alone. He worked eighty hours a week as a doctor and was at a loss for how to handle the situation.

Hal immediately went to assist Rick in any way he could.

Wanda recalls, "About a year had passed since Fred's death and I told my daughters that I was ready to get on with my life. Both girls were glad to hear it and encouraged me to start dating, but I didn't want to put them through the inconsistency of dating. I definitely didn't want to date anyone who had sons because I thought it could complicate things too much with my teenage girls, but I was open to developing friendships."

On one of Hal's trips to check on his friend, Rick asked how Wanda was getting along. Having spent so much time praying for Wanda before her husband died, Rick felt as though he knew her.

Hal gave him an update and Rick asked if he thought it would be okay to write her a letter, since they both had lost spouses. Hal relayed the request to Wanda and she consented.

Wanda continues, "Rick and I began corresponding. Soon, the letters turned to phone calls—lots of very long phone calls. In fact, Joanie, the social worker at the home, threatened to put me on phone restriction because after talking until the wee hours of the morning, I was having trouble concentrating and staying awake the next day!"

After another trip to visit Rick, Hal found out that his flight was cancelled due to an airline catastrophe. It was 4th of July weekend and getting a reservation on another airline was going to cost a lot more money, so Rick offered to drive Hal home.

After all, there was someone in Savannah he wanted to meet in person anyway.

On the drive to Savannah, Rick began to realize that he had fallen in love with Wanda over the phone. He also realized that he had no idea how tall she was, how much she weighed, or even what race she was. All he knew was that he loved her.

Rick and Wanda had a wonderful weekend—a 4th of July barbecue, time at the beach, and much more talking. Wanda also fell in love with Rick's "all-girl" family. They both came away with the certainty that they were in love and were going to be married. So Rick invited Wanda to come to Ohio and meet his family.

Again, they had a wonderful time together. As Rick drove Wanda to the airport to return to Savannah, he realized that he had not given her an engagement ring. So they stopped by a mall, picked out a ring, and Wanda returned home engaged.

For years, Rick had taken his family to Hilton Head for a week at the end of the summer. This year, he invited Wanda and her girls to come along. He also suggested that they get married while they were there. Wanda said she'd love to join him, but that she needed to discuss it with her daughters.

After Candice, Courtney, and Wanda all agreed that the wedding plans were a wonderful idea, Wanda called Rick and told him the good news. They made the necessary preparations and, with all seven girls in attendance, they were married at Hilton Head Beach.

Wanda and her girls moved to Ohio where she delights in homeschooling all seven of their girls. She also runs their match-made-in-heaven household with amazing efficiency.

In addition, Rick and Wanda have recently become foster parents to five African-American children, all under the age of five. The youngest two are nine-month-old twins.

❀ ❀ ❀

I have been young, and now am old; yet I have never seen the righteous forsaken, nor his descendants begging bread. He is ever merciful, and lends; And his descendents are blessed.

PSALM 37:25–26

Somebody's Knockin'

Her instructions began. "I'll hold onto your elbow and you'll just guide me to the restroom. When we arrive, I'll need for you to lead me inside and tell me where everything is. That's it."

As we got to the rest room, I swung open the door with my left hip, as Terri was holding onto my right elbow.

"Hang on just a second, Terri, I'm trying to find the light switch," I proudly informed her.

"For whom?" she asked as she laughed. I wondered how many more references to vision I could make in one day!

We wrote five songs that first day and Terri memorized all of the lyrics and music that day and recorded them on a cassette work tape before we parted ways. I was amazed.

She is a great singer, a fabulous songwriter, a wife, mom, a wonderful cook, and her humor is unmatched. I love Terri Gibbs with all of my heart and consider her to be my sister and good friend.

❀ ❀ ❀

IN WHAT SEEMED TO BE SUCH A SHORT TIME, Terri Gibbs had made a huge splash in the country music industry. Along with her success came all the material possessions she could have imagined, including her dream home.

In November of 1986, and only six years after her debut album, Terri found herself in the midst of change. She was feeling led to make the change from singing country music to singing Christian music. That's when she landed a deal with Word Records.

Terri was going through several transitions at that time. She was trying to sell her dream home because she wasn't working as much as she had been and could no longer keep up the payments. She was also in the process of changing management. She knew the Lord was leading her to make all of these decisions, yet with so many changes happening at once, she was beginning to deal with depression and uncertainty.

Terri recalls, "For several months, I had been attending a Bible study at the Koinonia Bookstore every Tuesday morning. It was designed to meet the needs of people in the music industry. The singing was great, the teaching was fabulous, and then there was always a time for prayer requests. I really loved going because it was a safe place to openly share your heart with people you could trust.

"The night before one particular day of Bible study, I had been very restless. The weight of all the changes, particularly having to give up my home, had left me struggling against an ever-present tendency to feel depressed. I had awakened several times during the previous night and had found comfort reading my Braille Bible and listening to teaching tapes.

"The next morning, because I hadn't slept well, I almost didn't go to the Bible study. But I was so miserable I knew that I needed to make the effort. I also had a meeting with Word at 11 A.M. and knew I needed to get myself together for that, as well.

"Being extremely shy, I had never opened up and shared anything with my friends at the Bible study. Yet, several times during the session that day, I felt the Lord prompting me to ask them to pray for me. Still not confident enough to open up to them, I refused God's urging several more times."

After the prayer requests had all been addressed, the worship leader dismissed everyone. As everyone stood to leave, however, the leader said, "Wait just a minute, everybody. I believe the Lord just showed me that Terri needs us to pray for her."

"I was totally overwhelmed. I couldn't believe that God was willing to do for me what I was unable to do for myself. I began to cry profusely. At that point everyone gathered around me and began to pray for me. One of the women there told me that she could see a wall around me. The wall was so high that I couldn't get over it and it was so wide that I couldn't go around it. But she also saw that God was going to walk me right through it! This was the encouragement that I needed during such a difficult time."

A few weeks later, Terri was over helping her girlfriend Teresa, who was writing an anniversary song for her parents. While together that day, they discovered their mutual love for Monopoly. Teresa told Terri that her family used to play it all the time, but because her brother David always beat everyone, they hadn't played in a while.

The person who was buying Terri's house was coming by the next evening to assess the property. For obvious reasons, she didn't want to be there, so she made plans to go play Monopoly with Teresa and her family.

That was the first time she met David.

She definitely feels like she won that Monopoly game because a year later, Terri and David were married. She may not have landed on Boardwalk or Park Place, but she came out the winner! Terri and David now have a son, David, Jr.

Terri explains, "As I was avoiding having to witness losing my prized house, God was already replacing it with something so much more meaningful. I learned that God is truly a God who works miracles in all areas of our lives, and sometimes He blesses us in the most unusual ways."

I will both lie down in peace, and sleep; for You alone, O LORD, make me dwell in safety.

PSALM 4:8

I Can Do All Things
through Christ

MARK PRICE GRADUATED FROM GEORGIA TECH, where he led his team to their first ACC championship game. He was drafted by the Cleveland Cavaliers and played in the NBA for nine years. He retired in 1999 and has accepted a position as an assistant coach at his alma mater, Georgia Tech. He and his wife Laura have four children.

Mark and I became friends while attending the same church. We found we have a mutual love for music. I adore Mark and his wife Laura and was grateful to interview him by phone just after the birth of their fourth child.

For as long as he can remember, Mark has had a passion for basketball. Throughout his childhood and adolescence, Mark's dad, Dennis, who had been a basketball coach at Sam Houston State University and the University of Oklahoma, as well as an assistant coach with the Phoenix Suns, constantly worked with Mark and his two brothers to perfect their game.

All of his hard work paid off when Mark earned a scholarship to Georgia Tech. Even though he was one of the smallest players to ever play the game, he consistently set records and played beyond what most considered his maximum potential. Mark led the Georgia Tech Yellow Jackets to their first ACC tournament championship in 1985.

There were many skeptics who openly voiced their doubts about Mark's chances to make it professionally in the National Basketball League. Yet upon graduating from Georgia Tech, he was drafted by the Cleveland Cavaliers.

Mark received a two-year contract. Many people told Mark that he'd better enjoy those two years because they predicted his tenure would be short-lived.

When he reported for his first year, Mark had no idea what to expect. Embarking on a new phase of his career was tough enough, but within the first month he had to undergo an emergency appendectomy. It knocked him out for a month of the season.

Following his recovery period, Mark returned to the game. The position he was assigned to play was backup to the veteran point guard, John Bagley. After all was said and done, Mark ended up having a pretty bad first season and he really didn't know what to anticipate for the upcoming year.

Mark explains, "Then the Cavaliers drafted a new point guard. Typically, a team never keeps three point guards and since I wasn't already the starter, the writing seemed to be on the wall that I would be the player to be let go. But I just continued to trust God and work hard. I prayed about my situation and, having faith in God to work things out, I left my future in the hands of the Lord.

"There wasn't anything I could do about the situation except to work hard and improve my game. All summer long I worked out, trying to get myself back in shape so I could show the powers that be that I was worth keeping. I wanted them to see all of the qualities that I had not been able to demonstrate that first year."

About a week before Mark was to come back to camp, the Cavaliers suddenly traded their point guard starter, John Bagley, to another team. The player they had drafted to replace John was still negotiating his contract and wasn't due to arrive at camp for about two weeks.

In two weeks, the Cavaliers went from having potentially three point guards to only having Mark. This gave Mark the opportunity for which he had prayed—to show them his talents as a player. Mark was in excellent condition and was playing great.

136

The new player finally arrived, but he couldn't beat Mark out for the spot. Halfway through the season, the Cavaliers traded the new player because they were so pleased with the job Mark was doing. Mark had earned the starting spot.

In a situation that had not looked promising at all, Mark did all he could do, then God intervened and answered Mark's prayer. The result was what most would consider miraculous.

Mark continued to play for Cleveland for nine years. During that time, he made the All-Star Team four times and played with the Dream Team twice. He was the NBA's Long Distance Shootout Winner during All-Star Weekend in 1993 and 1994. He has seen action in forty-seven play-off games and, with a .907 percentage, still holds the all-time NBA record for free throws.

Mark retired from basketball in 1999. Thirteen years after his collegiate career ended and following in the footsteps of his dad, Mark Price is returning to Georgia Tech as an assistant basketball coach. Coaching will give him more time at home with his wife and children.

Anytime I've heard Mark Price speak or seen an autograph bearing his signature, he always includes one particular scripture verse. Looking back over Mark's amazingly successful career and seeing how he has excelled in every area of influence, it's easy to understand why he always so eagerly points to the passage that says:

❁ ❁ ❁

I can do all things through Christ which strengthens me.

Philippians 4:13

THE PRINCE

An award-winning lyricist, author, and speaker, Claire Cloninger is one of the most profound and gifted talents of our time.

She is a four-time Gospel Music Association Dove winner, whose songs have been recorded by Amy Grant, Sandi Patty, Wayne Watson, and B.J. Thomas. Claire has written nineteen seasonal musicals for church choir including *The Gift of Christmas, He's Alive, A Son! A Savior,* and *My Utmost for His Highest.*

Claire's inspirational books include *A Place Called Simplicity, Postcards from Heaven, Postcards for People Who Hurt, Postcards for People in Love, When the Glass Slipper Doesn't Fit, Faithfully Fit,* and her most recent release, *Abba Father.*

As a sought-after speaker for women's retreats and conferences, Claire is on the go almost every weekend.

When she's home, Claire lives with her husband, Spike, in a log cabin retreat, nestled on the banks of a river in Baldwin County, Alabama. They have two sons, both married and each having one daughter. Spending time with her granddaughters has become the joy of her life and something she cherishes and looks forward to at every opportunity.

I met Claire when she judged my song in the competition at the Christian Artists Music Seminar in Estes Park, Colorado. I have learned much of what I know about songwriting both from Claire directly and from studying her lyrics. She's a master craftswoman.

❀ ❀ ❀

CLAIRE HAS TWO SISTERS. The three of them and their families have always been very close. When Claire's oldest sister, Alix, was diagnosed with a rare type of nonsmoker's lung cancer, the family was devastated. The doctors informed Claire and her family that even if they had spotted it when the first cancerous cell appeared, it still would have probably been impossible to treat successfully. For this type of cancer, which spreads through the lungs with a honeycomb-type effect, there was simply no effective type of treatment.

The prognosis was terminal.

Claire and the rest of her family tried to spend as much time as possible with Alix. Watching her struggle to do the simple things, like talking, laughing, and breathing, was difficult for everyone close to her.

They prayed for a miracle. They put her name on prayer lists throughout the country. They had everyone they knew agree in prayer with them, asking God to heal her.

But finally, Alix lost her battle with cancer.

Alix's daughter, Jeanne, read a book on how to tell her five-year-old, Mary Grace, that her grandmother had died. It recommended straightforward honesty.

She began. "Mary Grace, you know Momee has been sick for a long time."

Mary Grace nodded her head affirmatively.

"Well, honey, last night your Momee died and went to heaven."

As Mary Grace began to cry, Jeanne picked her up and held her. She wiped her tears away and Jeanne began to explain further.

"Remember how Momee hasn't been able to eat or drink much of anything?"

Mary Grace, still whimpering, nodded her head.

"And remember how Momee coughed all of the time and had trouble talking and laughing?"

In her soft little voice, Mary Grace responded, "Yes."

Jeanne explained, "Well, now she can jump and laugh and talk. She's dancing with Jesus and she's so happy."

With that, Mary Grace spoke with great enthusiasm, "Then I'm glad, Mama. Aren't you glad?"

Gently, Jeanne said, "Yes, honey, I'm glad. And now I've got to go somewhere with Pops."

"Where are you going?" Mary Grace inquired.

"I've got to go and pick out the bed that Momee is going to rest in."

"You mean like Snow White!" Mary Grace said with great enthusiasm.

Jeanne didn't want Mary Grace to expect her grandmother to wake up and come back like Snow White, so she answered carefully.

"Yes, just like Snow White, Mary Grace. Except that Snow White wasn't really dead, honey, and Momee *is* really dead. So there won't be a handsome prince to wake her up."

Later, as Jeanne was telling Claire about her conversation with Mary Grace, the truth hit them both at once. They looked at each other and said at the same time, "Yes, there is a prince! Alix was kissed and awakened by the Prince of Peace and now she's in a place where she'll live happily ever after."

❀ ❀ ❀

And His name will be called Wonderful, Counselor, Mighty God, Everlasting Father, Prince of Peace.

ISAIAH 9:6

THE YOGURT SHOP

IT WAS MY FIRST DAY AS A VOLUNTEER at the Crisis Pregnancy Center. I had been through all the training classes, but nothing could have prepared me for what was about to happen.

I heard the front door to the office open and then the bell at our sliding window sounded, alerting us that our 2 P.M. appointment had arrived. As I slid open the window that separated our office area from the reception room, I saw my first clients. He was in his late twenties, a midget who walked with a cane and had a deformed arm. The girl looked about seventeen, very frail, and never made eye contact. He was the spokesperson.

"We're here for abortion information," he said.

I handed him a form to complete, told him to let us know when he had finished it, and closed the window.

I was nervous. I knew I was about to provide a great service, but it was not what they were expecting. Our program was one that educated women about abortion alternatives. I realized that he had already made up his mind before they came in that the girl was going to have an abortion. I was quickly beginning to dread the whole situation.

He finished filling out the form, and I asked the young woman to give me a urine sample. Then I told them we'd like for them to watch a short film while I processed the free pregnancy test.

The film showed the various stages of pregnancy. For me, this was the thing that most impressed me when I was doing my training. Prior to seeing the film, I had not realized that a baby had a heartbeat three weeks after conception. Nor did I know that it had viable brain waves, a skeletal structure, and all of its organs at six weeks. If the baby is genetically predisposed to diabetes, or any other diseases, it's all locked in by that stage. I guess it was during my first look at that film when it hit me that the fetus is a baby. All the parts are there; it just continues to grow. Abortion really does stop a beating heart.

I had just completed her pregnancy test—it was positive; she was four months pregnant—when suddenly, I heard the door to the room where they were watching the film forcefully fling open. The man was limping toward me with his cane pointed at my face and screaming obscenities.

"How dare you show her this film! We're here for an abortion!"

The girl was crying hysterically. The man said his girlfriend had a venereal disease, which meant that if she went to term, she would have to have a C-section and they could not afford that. He said he didn't want to take a chance on bringing a deformed child into the world. He was adamant. They wanted an abortion.

I tried to calm them. I wanted them to know we would help in any way we could. We would provide food, shelter, baby clothes, furniture, medical assistance, help if they wanted to keep their baby, referrals to adoption services if they wanted to place their baby. But, he was unyielding and they stormed out the door.

Over the next few weeks I tried to reach them again and again. Finally, their phone was disconnected and I never did get through to them. I kept having mental replays of his anger and her tears. I couldn't even let myself think about their baby.

Several years later, I was en route from Atlanta to Nashville and decided to swing by a yogurt shop and get a frozen yogurt for the road. I had purchased my treat and was turning to exit when an adorable little boy of about three or so wedged himself between me and the door. He had beautiful dark hair and playful brown eyes. His cheeks were rosy red and his smile lit up the room. I gazed down at him, gave him a wink, and said, "What are you doin', big guy?" He giggled back at me.

A masculine voice from over my shoulder beckoned his young son away from the door. Now free to open the door, I turned to catch one more glance of the beautiful boy who had momentarily held me captive. Much to my surprise, I saw that his father was the midget with the deformed arm and the cane.

A rush of heat consumed me as I realized the couple I had seen that day had decided not to get an abortion. An avalanche of thoughts reeled through my head—*but, they were so mad at me. He said they were definitely going through with it.* I remembered the cane being pointed in my face and the man's jugular veins popping out of his neck as he screamed at me.

Too stunned to respond or to remind him of our former encounter, I walked slowly to my car. What a gift God had just given me. I took a slow, smooth taste of my yogurt. Mixed with its sweet taste was the salt from the tears pouring down my face.

I remembered the verse in Proverbs which says, "God can turn the hearts of kings." I doubted that the father of the little boy was royalty, but based on my last encounter with him, I believe God had definitely moved to change his heart!

I was ashamed that I had conceded failure in this situation and I was glad that God hadn't given up as easily as I had.

I thought of Sunday school songs like "Jesus Loves Me," "God Can Do Anything But Fail," and "Jesus Loves the Little Children." I hoped that the little boy would have a chance to know God and how much He loves him. In consideration of what I had just experienced, I was sure God would orchestrate such an encounter. The truth of God's sovereignty and His uncompromising ability to rule the universe flooded my heart.

God entrusts us with many opportunities in life. Sometimes we will never know the results or see the impact we have on other people. But occasionally we do get the great gift of a glimpse. For me, the yogurt shop encounter was one of those times.

❀ ❀ ❀

Before I formed you in your mother's womb I knew you.

JEREMIAH 1:5

143

THE WINDOWS AND DOORS
OF HEAVEN

It is difficult to hear songs like "Up, Up and Away," "The Age of Aquarius," or "One Less Bell" without envisioning The 5th Dimension and the beautiful face and voice of their original female singer, Florence LaRue.

Not only is she a six-time Grammy Award winner for her accomplishments in the music industry, Florence has also made her mark and realized many of her dreams in the acting world. In addition to many other projects, Florence has been in a movie-of-the-week and has toured with the Tony Award winning musical *Ain't Misbehavin'*.

She has also received many other personal honors and awards. In 1986, Florence was named Woman of the Year by The City of Hope and received their prestigious Spirit of Life Award. This resulted in a research fellowship in her name for the purpose of the extensive study and treatment of gynecological cancer.

Florence is a member of the Board of Directors of the Christian Entertainment Fellowship. She is also a very active member of the Celebrity Action Council, which is made up of celebrities who offer encouragement, support, and ministry to women in a rehabilitative residency program at the Ann Douglas Center.

After being named one of the ten most beautiful women in the world of entertainment, along with the likes of Sophia Loren and Lena Horne, Florence was asked how she felt about the honor: "Naturally, I'm thrilled, but I believe that beauty comes from within. Mainly what I see when I look in the mirror is someone who tries to look her best and stay healthy— mentally, physically, and spiritually."

With a bachelor's degree in education, Florence has always been a teacher at heart and is involved in many civic activities, particularly those involving abused children.

She strongly believes that education coupled with spiritual guidance holds the key to healing, which can precipitate a life filled with more freedom and fullness. Her desire is to open centers all around the country that will house and counsel abused children, as well as their emotionally conflicted parents.

I met Florence by phone through our mutual friend, Zoro the drummer. She was soft-spoken, kind, and very accommodating. When the interview was completed, we prayed together, and I could sense her deep commitment and love for our Lord.

❁ ❁ ❁

FLORENCE HAS BEEN A CHRISTIAN since she was a child. As long as she can remember, God has been an intimate part of her life and it has been her heart's desire to follow Him in all phases and facets of her life.

As Florence began making a substantial living with The 5th Dimension, she prided herself in the fact that she was never frivolous with her money. She bought a nice home, but not an extravagant one. She never hired limousines. Florence wasn't selfish, but shared her money with her family by treating her dad and sisters to trips and cruises. She also sent her son to a private school.

The one thing she had not learned about, however, was investment strategies and tax shelters. In her first year with the group, she was proud of the fact that she was able to save $50,000. Yet, with all her efforts to be frugal, she ended up having a tax bill that wiped out every penny she had put away.

"Another thing I had failed to do" Florence recalls, "was to prepare for the leaner times. As the Bible teaches in Proverbs 6:6-8, "Go to the ant; consider her ways and be wise! Which having no chief, overseer or ruler, provides her food in the summer and gathers her supplies in the harvest."

Even with all of her career success and her prudent spending habits, there came a time when Florence found herself in a financial slump, bringing about a serious cash flow problem.

She continues, "I had been convicted for some time that tithing ten percent of my income was not only a privilege but, according to God's word, it was a requirement. I had studied Proverbs 3:9 which says, "Honor the LORD with your capital and sufficiency and with the first fruits of all your income."

As Florence sat in church one Sunday, the offering plates were beginning to make their way down the aisles and were methodically heading in the direction of her pew. She was in a dilemma. She needed to pay her utility bills and wanted to keep her good credit.

I prayed silently, "Lord, I need to pay my utilities and I know You're always there, so I'll pay You next week."

Immediately, she heard the reply, "First fruits."

In a slow, hesitant way, Florence wrote out her tithe check. After putting the check into the plate, she didn't think about it anymore. She had been obedient and it was up to God to take care of her needs.

Florence recalls, "The next week, I received a residual check from a recording I had done years before. The check was totally unexpected. Not only did it cover my utilities, but it was also about five times more than I needed. God had provided, with money to spare."

"That experience built my faith and I never wonder anymore about *how* God will do what I know He will do. I learned that if

I'm obedient to God by giving Him the first ten percent of my income, my needs will always be met. I have also learned to be a good steward of the remainder of my income. If we don't have money, we can't bless others.

"God wants His children to have money, but He wants us to be wise and to be good stewards. I remember that day in my life when my perspective on money was permanently put into its proper place. I decided to give to God from my first fruits without question, and in doing so, He opened the windows and doors of heaven and I experienced the blessings of God."

❀ ❀ ❀

"Bring all the tithes into the storehouse, that there may be food in My house, and try Me in this," says the LORD of hosts, "If I will not open the windows of heaven and pour out for you such a blessing that there will not be room enough to receive it."

MALACHI 3:10

NICE TO MEET YOU, LORD!

Miguel Melendez is president of the Melendez Entertainment Group. Among others, he manages R&B singing sensation Deborah Cox and former New Kids on the Block now solo artist Jordan Knight. During his successful career in management, Miguel has also been involved with the careers of Vanessa Williams, Boyz 2 Men, and Janet Jackson.

I met Miguel over the phone while he was accompanying Jordan Knight on tour for his new record. We had a great conversation and have since become email pals.

❋ ❋ ❋

MIGUEL WAS BORN AND RAISED A CATHOLIC. Although he was reared in a good family and attended church on a fairly regular basis, it was only about ten months ago that Miguel Melendez personally accepted Jesus Christ as his Savior.

The decision to surrender his life to Christ completely changed him. He began to pray and study the Bible, trying to learn God's ways, rather than continuing to live his life by the world's standards. He would soon learn that in most cases, the two dynamics are in direct opposition to each other. This was going to take some getting used to.

Miguel had a great job as a junior partner at a management company called South Paw. The company was responsible for overseeing the careers of many noted artists, including Boyz 2 Men, Vanessa Williams, and Janet Jackson.

Almost immediately after accepting Christ, Miguel felt God telling him to put in his notice and open his own company.

At first, Miguel hoped he was hearing the echo of God telling someone *else* to quit their job. Surely this request was not for him. He loved his job, a place where he had security, position, and a bright future.

But the prompting continued and, in fact, intensified—*Delay no longer!*

Miguel explains, "In church that Sunday, my pastor, Bishop Clarence McClendon, spoke about how the Holy Spirit moves in our lives. He said some people call it a gut feeling, but it is actually the movement of God. Bishop McClendon referred to the passage in Luke 1 where, through an angel, God tells Mary she's been chosen to give birth to Jesus.

"I was encouraged by my pastor's message and although I still had some reservations, the word of God strengthened me. I knew if God was leading me to make this move, He would also provide and give me favor in the transition."

"I began to pray. I voiced my concerns to God, telling Him that I would need $6,000 to open my company. I had a tax refund coming, but was only getting back $1,500. So I told God that I would be glad to start my own company, but God would have to provide the money I needed.

Soon after that, my tax refund arrived. Accompanying it was a letter explaining that an error had been made—instead of $1,500 the check was for $5,800."

In church the next Sunday, Miguel's girlfriend explained tithing to him and told him how God's word instructs us to give Him ten percent of all of our earnings. Whoa! Miguel thought ten percent was a little steep. He said he could live with five percent, but ten seemed a little unreasonable. His girlfriend told him that he needed to give what was in his heart, but that God says to give ten percent. She also told him that God loves a *cheerful* giver.

"As the praise and worship began, my heart began to spill over with gratitude and joy for my newfound relationship with Jesus.

My heart began to soften. I tore up my check for five percent, wrote a new one for ten percent, and actually felt great about it!

"From there, I put in my notice and started my new company. All three of my clients—Jordan Knight, Deborah Cox, and Robin Thicke—left with me."

Deborah Cox's first single from her new record stayed at #1 on the Billboard charts for fourteen weeks. Jordan Knight's new record and video were released and are now receiving rave reviews.

Before her record came out, Deborah, her producers, and Miguel took the record to church and had the congregation pray over it. After the huge success of the single, Deborah and Miguel had a meeting with her record company. They said, "The single is good, but you guys have something going for you besides that."

They both responded in unison, "God!"

Miguel continues, "I am experiencing tremendous favor in all facets of my business, "I'm learning that if you put your trust in God and go for the things He puts in your heart, everything will work out.

"Even though it has seemed like a whirlwind since I invited Jesus into my life, this experience has been far removed from the life of power and position I held ten months ago. When I asked Jesus into my life, it was like I said, 'I accept You as my Savior and Lord. It's nice to meet You, Lord!'

"As we are faithful with the small things in life, God is faithful to open up more and more doors and take us to places we never thought possible."

❀ ❀ ❀

He who is faithful over the small things will be faithful over much.

LUKE 16:10

150

DETERMINED TO FOLLOW GOD

Browsing through any bookstore, it would not be unusual to see Zoro's face gracing the covers of teen magazines, music magazines, and human-interest magazines alike. In fact he was just voted the Best R&B Drummer in the *Modern Drummer* and *Drum Magazine's* reader's poll.

Zoro has authored several books including *The Commandments of R&B Drumming*, *The Master's Plan*, (a book he uses in his ministry work), and *If I Can Dream* (a tool for his motivational speaking and seminar work).

Zoro has a passion for young people and for becoming involved in film projects that can make a difference.

❀ ❀ ❀

IN 1993, ZORO WAS CONSIDERED one of the hottest, most well respected and sought-after drummers in the music business. He had a job he loved and was making a good income. He had a beautiful wife, cars, clothes, and his dream home. He was a faithful husband and loved the Lord with all of his heart. Zoro was experiencing all the good things in life and life could not have been better.

His wife was traveling with him as he toured that year with Bobby Brown, New Edition, and Lenny Kravitz. Zoro always tries to bring her on his tours as an assistant road manager or a wardrobe person. It was a great opportunity for them to see the world together.

Just as both of these tours ended, Zoro was given an invitation to join a European tour with French singer/supermodel Vanessa Paradis, an act that Lenny Kravitz had produced. Vanessa was well known as the Madonna of France. The only drawback was that the tour would last for six months and there wasn't a position open for Zoro's wife. After discussing it, however, they decided it was a good opportunity for him and that he should go anyway. He left for Europe and his wife stayed home.

Over the weeks to come, Zoro and his wife communicated regularly, and every week he sent home his paycheck so that she could pay all their bills and tithe to their church.

One day without warning, Zoro's wife called and informed him that she wanted a divorce. He was devastated.

There were still a few more weeks on the tour and Zoro decided to keep his commitment and finish the job. He was tormented as he tried to find answers to what had gone wrong.

"I lost weight and got down to 125 lbs.," Zoro confides, "I had always been thin, but this situation was really taking its toll on my health. I prayed constantly, asking God to intervene and perform a miracle that would restore my marriage. It was difficult for me to see beyond the immediate and believe there could be a positive resolution to such an impossible situation.

"I finished the tour and arrived home on my birthday. The first words out of my wife's mouth were that she was having an affair. The man had been staying in their house with her while I was away. She then informed me that she had secured a job with the Meatloaf tour and would be leaving immediately.

"Reviewing our bank account, I discovered that all of the money I had been sending home had been spent, with the exception of about $6,000. My wife had blown the rest of it on new clothes and entertainment.

"I also realized that she had not tithed on any of my paychecks. What I felt I owed God was exactly what I had left in the bank. Because I was a committed tither, I decided to write out my check. I knew that in doing so I would be virtually penniless, but I felt that God had blessed me with the tour, so it was the right thing to do."

As divorce proceedings began, Zoro and his wife split up their community property. Zoro gave her the house in Seattle and he kept the one in Los Angeles. He was determined to be kind and godly throughout the entire ordeal.

Zoro needed to find a gig, so when an opportunity to audition for Johnny Gill came about, he enthusiastically gave it his all. But someone else was hired.

"I continued to call out to God for hope and help. I had lost my wife, had no job and very little money. What else could possibly happen?

"Then the earthquake hit. My home and practically everything in it were completely destroyed. The few items that did survive were packed up in a U-haul and sold in a yard sale at my church for pennies.

"While my house was in disrepair, I rented a room in the home of an eighty-year-old prayer warrior from my church. I was literally living with the little old lady from Pasadena!"

As they got to know each other, he asked his landlady to pray with him about securing a job. He also let her know that he was afraid he might lose his credit. She began to pray and boldly stand against anything that would try to destroy Zoro's credit. She also asked God to provide a source of income for him.

Soon another job opportunity came along with Frankie Valli and the Four Seasons. Zoro knew all of their music. In preparation for the audition, he went over to his church and listened to many of their CDs. Before the audition, he did as he'd always done. He prayed that God would open the door if it was God's best for him, and to close the door if it was not in His plan.

He got the job!

Shortly after being hired by Frankie Valli and the Four Seasons, Zoro learned that the job with Johnny Gill would have ended after only two weeks. The Four Seasons gig was for much longer—definitely worth the wait.

Zoro's insurance adjuster contacted him regarding the property damage that had been incurred during the earthquake. Although Zoro suspected his coverage was insufficient, the adjuster informed him that his policy had covered everything. Zoro's house was completely rebuilt and restored. It was now better than it had been prior to the earthquake and all of the possessions he thought he had lost were fully replaced.

"Shortly after my divorce was final, I went on the road with Frankie Valli. God had restored my house, my finances, my health, and had given me a job. I was very grateful, but on the tour I frequently became lonely.

"I had numerous opportunities to meet women before and after all of their concerts, but that wasn't what I was looking for. I prayed that God would send me a wife I could love, honor, and spend the rest of my life with."

One day while at a hotel in Las Vegas, Zoro decided to go to an outlet mall to shop for a sports watch. As he entered the store, he noticed a very large, well-built man resembling a pirate. The man wore a sports watch and extended his wrist toward Zoro so he could check it out. Zoro admired the watch and a conversation ensued. The man's name was Frank. They chatted for quite sometime and realized they had something in common—they were both Christians.

Zoro walked Frank and his wife, Debbie, to their car. Frank told Zoro he wanted him to get up the next day at 7 A.M. and eat six boiled eggs. Then Zoro was to come to their house at 9:00 A.M. to work out. Zoro drove back to his hotel humming the theme song to *Rocky*!

He showed up at Frank and Debbie's the next day and they became instant friends. During Zoro's stint in Vegas, they ended up hanging out together for at least some portion of every day.

Frank encouraged Zoro to go before God and begin to thank

Him for sending a wife. Frank explained that we must have the faith to call what is not, as though it is.

That night, Zoro began to practice what Frank had suggested. He thanked God for sending him a wife. He thanked God for preparing him for her and her for him. He thanked God that her identity would be made known to him in God's perfect time. In the interim, he needed for God to strengthen him with the will to wait.

When it was time for Zoro to return to Los Angeles, Frank introduced him to Dennis, another bodybuilder friend of his in Los Angeles, and his wife, Anita. Anita and Dennis attended a small church. The Sunday after meeting Zoro, their pastor did a sermon on celibacy and the importance of waiting on God to send a mate. Anita realized that their pastor's daughter, Renee, who was twenty-eight years old, was traveling a similar path to Zoro's. She was committed to waiting on God, but she was seemingly unable to even meet anyone suitable to date.

"Anita decided to play cupid. She phoned me and told me she'd found my wife. I thought that was wonderful and wanted to meet her immediately. When we were introduced, there was an instant bonding. That night, Anita, Renee, and I went to hear a guest speaker at a church. On the ride home, Anita fell asleep. Renee and I talked for hours and listened to music.

"A week later, we went out on our first official date. Two weeks after that, I asked her to marry me. Four months later, we were married, and now four years later we just had our first child, Jarod Christopher.

"The Lord promises to restore all that has been lost or stolen from his children. I made a commitment to honor the Lord in all things and God has blessed me beyond all that I could ever ask or think!"

❀ ❀ ❀

So I will restore to you the years that the swarming locust has eaten, the crawling locust, the consuming locust, and the chewing locust, My great army which I sent among you. You shall eat in plenty and be satisfied, and praise the name of the LORD your God, who has dealt wondrously with you; and my people shall never be put to shame. Then you shall know that I am in the midst of Israel. I am the LORD your God and there is no other. My people shall never be put to shame.

JOEL 2:25–27

156

LIFE INSURANCE

In his youth, Lee Buck was a prize-winning boxer, an accomplished musician, and a Lieutenant in the Navy. Mr. Buck became Senior Vice President in charge of Marketing at New York Life Insurance, supervising twelve thousand agents and three hundred fifty offices in the United States and Canada. He left his position at New York Life to go into full-time ministry.

He's been on the board of directors of Faith Alive and the Walter Hoving Home, Regent University, and is the Director of Episcopal Renewal Ministries. He and his wife have raised four biological daughters and ten foster daughters. He is author of the best-selling book *Tapping Your Secret Source of Success.*

I caught an interview with Mr. Buck on the *Praise the Lord* television program on the Trinity Broadcasting Network. I found him to be so vibrant and interesting I wanted to try and contact him for my own interview. We did get in touch and our chat was immensely enjoyable. Mr. Buck is truly one of God's choice servants.

❁ ❁ ❁

SEVENTY-SIX YEARS AGO IN A SMALL TOWN in Michigan, Lee Buck was born into severe poverty. His family lived in a run-down tarpaper shack with dirt floors. They burned wood in an oil barrel for heat. Lee's older brother was eighteen when Lee was born, so he never really got to know him. His father died when Lee was three, leaving him, his mother, and his younger brother to struggle on their own.

At thirteen, Lee found his older brother's saxophone under the bed and learned how to play it. His mother ran a beer joint, and Lee quickly learned he could make a decent living playing a horn. One night, a factory worker stuffed a dollar bill down into his sax. In those days, a dollar would buy ten loaves of bread or ten quarts of milk. Lee immediately began playing five nights a week around the area.

Because he worked so much, Lee couldn't participate in any of the sports programs at school. Instead, he joined a boxing league and learned that he was quite good at fighting.

There was a boxing club around the corner from the beer joint. Lee could make ten dollars by going three rounds. He had thirty fights and eighteen knock-outs in his young career. At one point, he thought he might pursue becoming the world's most successful boxer, but the last time he fought, he got creamed and decided to stay with his original plan of becoming the world's most famous musician.

Although he played the sax all through college, after he married, Lee only continued playing for five more years. Instead, he served in World War II and in the Korean War. He also earned three college degrees.

Then Lee went to work in the insurance business and quickly moved up the ranks of the company. He and his family moved into a house in New Canaan, Connecticut, that had tennis courts, a swimming pool, a stable with three horses, and a variety of other amenities any person could possibly want. By then Lee was the Vice President of Marketing for New York Life Insurance Company. He was living the good life.

Audrey, his wife, had been attending a Bible study for quite some time, but Lee was a "Sunday-only" kind of guy. Church was a social event that Lee considered boring and a chore.

"One evening, Audrey told me that she had given her heart to

Jesus at a Bible study. She wanted me to go with her to hear a missionary speak at a local parish."

Lee agreed to go.

"When we walked into the church, I noticed that everyone was up at the front and it was very noisy. I was accustomed to more reverence in a church service. When the music began, the congregation clapped and some of them even lifted their hands. I stood up with them, but thought the whole service was ridiculous."

"The missionary told the congregation about the many miracles that he had seen on the mission field. He said that he had witnessed healing of the sick and raising of the dead. By this time, I wanted to scream and wondered what in the world Audrey had gotten into."

"After the missionary concluded, the priest gave an altar call. I didn't know what an altar call was, but I kept noticing that as the people went forward, they seemed to disappear. Out of curiosity, I went up. I got closer and noticed that they were all kneeling, so I followed their lead. Next, I saw that this missionary was laying his hands on top of the people's heads.

Now, in those days, real men used "a little dab'll do ya." But Lee had figured out that his wife's hair spray would do the job without all of the grease. He knew if the priest touched his hair, he would be found out!

"When the priest laid hands on me, I stepped over the altar rail, ready to deck him, but a vision flashed through my mind." It was a headline of *The New York Times*:

"Insurance Executive Jailed for Decking Priest!"

Lee yelled at his wife so loudly that everyone could hear him: "Audrey, this is a hoax and I'm going home. You can stay if you want, but I'm leaving!" Well, Audrey wasn't about to leave, and he couldn't go either, because she had the car keys.

Eight weeks later, they visited another church. Lee hadn't shed a tear since he was eight years old, but as he entered the building, he suddenly began to weep. He was embarrassed that he was crying and couldn't figure out what was happening to him.

Lee sat in a corner and continued to cry for three more hours. Finally, at the end of the evening, he knew what he needed to do. He got down on his knees in front of everyone there and said, "Dear Lord Jesus, I guess I'm not much good, but if you want me, I'm yours."

That prayer changed his life forever.

Soon after, the pastor of the church—Lee and Audrey were now members—asked him if he would give his testimony. Lee didn't know what a testimony was, but because he had been speaking all his life, he agreed to do it. The pastor told him that all he had to do was tell the congregation how he came to know Jesus.

Lee told his pastor he thought that was a private matter. His pastor responded by telling Lee that his experience might have been *personal*, but it was not *private*. He said if it's *private*, you must not have really done it.

Lee decided to give his testimony.

He was expected to keep his testimony under ten minutes, but Lee gave his account in two minutes. Three young men gave their lives to Christ that night.

This experience set Lee on fire with the desire to share the gospel with everyone he possibly could. He decided he would be willing to talk about the Lord to any person put in his path. He could tell them about the kind of life insurance that is eternal.

He shared the gospel on the train as he rode in to work. At one point, *The New York Times* wrote an article on him, entitled "The Railroad Evangelist." After the article came out, some passengers were almost afraid to sit next to him.

Today women often approach him, asking if he can get their husbands saved. He is always quick to point out, however, that it is the Holy Spirit that prepares hearts to be open to salvation, and not him.

"Recently, while speaking at the New Covenant Church in Winter Springs, Florida, a woman named Martha approached me with a request to speak with her seventy-three-year-old father who was dying of cancer. Martha had done everything she knew to do to lead her father to the Lord, but her father wanted no part of it."

After church the next day, Lee and his wife, along with Martha and her mother, drove about an hour and a half to meet Nick, Martha's dad. Lee quickly assessed that he and Nick had a lot in common. They talked for a couple of hours about World War II, the Navy, and serving in the South Pacific.

Finally, Lee said, "You know, Nick, it seems to me that with all that you know and with all that you are, and the fact that you're going to die, I think it's time for you and me to pray together." Without hesitation, Nick agreed.

Lee began and Nick repeated after him, "Dear Lord Jesus, I confess to you that I'm a sinner. I'm sorry for my sins. Forgive me. LORD Jesus, I receive You into my heart as my Lord and Savior." With that, Nick began to cry.

A half an hour later, the rest of the family returned and Lee told Nick that he needed to tell his family what had happened. Nick smiled from ear to ear and said, "Okay, I did it!" There was great rejoicing in their home that day.

Through the years, Lee has spoken at over six hundred Episcopal Churches and dozens of others. He preaches throughout the world and estimates that he has had the opportunity to lead between 300,000 and 350,000 people to the Lord. He will continue devoting all of his efforts toward leading people to accept the "life insurance" that is offered to them through faith in Jesus.

❀ ❀ ❀

Therefore, having been justified by faith, we have peace with God through our Lord Jesus Christ, through whom also we have access by faith into this grace in which we stand and rejoice in hope of the glory of God.

STANDING
ON THE PROMISES

With hits like "Uneasy Rider," "The South's Gonna Do It," and "Long Haired Country Boy," multi-platinum country/blue-grass performer Charlie Daniels' career spans over four decades. His signature song, "The Devil Went Down to Georgia," became a platinum single, topped both the country and pop charts, won a Grammy, earned three Country Music Association trophies, became the lead song in the film *Urban Cowboy*, and propelled his *Million Miles Reflection* album to triple platinum sales.

Charlie called me from his bus while out on tour. He was down to earth and easy to talk to. At the end of our conversation I prayed for Charlie and he in return prayed for me.

❀ ❀ ❀

ONE OF THE MOST LIFE-CHANGING EXPERIENCES Charlie Daniels has ever had occurred several years ago while touring out on the road.

Hazel, his wife of thirty-five years, travels with him everywhere he goes. She had been experiencing severe back pain and had consulted with chiropractors, an osteopath, and an orthopedic surgeon. None of them had been able to pinpoint the cause of her back problem.

The last date before the end of the tour was a performance at

Farm Aid with Willie Nelson. After that they would be headed for home.

When Charlie finished his last show the night before doing Farm Aid, Hazel was in excruciating pain. Charlie wanted to take her to the hospital but she wanted to wait until they returned home to Nashville.

Charlie won out and he took her to a local hospital in Three Rivers, Michigan. After running a battery of tests, the doctors concluded that she had a gynecological problem, but they wouldn't be able to determine the specifics of her trouble until they did exploratory surgery.

Hazel didn't want to have surgery away from home, so she stayed in the hospital while Charlie sang at Farm Aid. After his performance, Charlie chartered an ambulance plane and flew Hazel back to Nashville. Hazel was immediately transported to Baptist Hospital and her surgery was scheduled for the following day.

"I left the hospital to go home, shower, and change clothes," Charlie began. "My love for my wife is very strong and, while driving home, I began to thank God for her and pray for the love of my life.

"I began to engage in spiritual warfare against the illness that was causing Hazel's problem. I told Satan that he couldn't have Hazel. I commanded Satan to take his hands off of her. I continued to rebuke Hazel's problem and called upon the Lord to heal her and restore her to perfect and whole health."

Charlie continued, "I returned to the hospital. After bringing my cares and concerns before the throne of God, I felt confident that the outcome from Hazel's surgery would be fine. One particular verse kept running through my mind: "Be anxious for nothing, but in everything by prayer and supplication with thanksgiving make your needs known to God; and the peace that passes all understanding will guard your hearts and minds through Christ Jesus." (Philippians 4: 6-7)

"The next morning before Hazel underwent her procedure, I told her that if she was holding onto anything in her heart against anybody or had any sin issues she was struggling with, that God wanted her to let go of it. I didn't want anything to prohibit God from intervening with supernatural power and to render a total and complete healing!"

Hazel told Charlie she didn't think she was holding onto anything unforgiven and that she, too, had asked God to provide wisdom for her surgeons and complete healing for her ailment.

The doctors wheeled Hazel down the hall for her surgery, which lasted several hours. After the procedure had been completed, the surgeons came out to speak with Charlie. They informed him that the situation had been extremely serious, but that everything was going to be fine.

Charlie already knew everything was going to be okay, but he rejoiced to hear his expectations confirmed by the attending physicians. Charlie had taken a stand against Satan who comes to steal, kill, and destroy our lives.

Hazel recovered in record time and Charlie's faith in the Lord was increased from having gone through the experience.

"When your back is to the wall, God's word has over 7,000 promises to stand on," Charlie shared. "Throughout my life, I've learned to do three things well: love my wife and family, sing and play the fool out of a fiddle, and experience the fullness of God by standing on His promises."

❀ ❀ ❀

Finally, my brethren, be strong in the Lord and in the power of His might. Put on the whole armor of God, that you may be able to stand against the wiles of the devil. For we do not wrestle against flesh and blood, but against principalities, against powers, against the rulers of the darkness of this age, against spiritual hosts of wickedness in the heavenly places. Therefore take up the whole armor of God, that you may be able to withstand in the evil day, and having done all, to stand. Stand therefore, having girded your waist with truth, having put on the breastplate of righteousness, and having shod your feet within the preparation of the gospel of peace; above all, taking the shield of faith with which you will be able to quench all the fiery darts of the wicked one. And take the helmet of salvation, and the sword of the Spirit, which is the word of God; praying always with all prayer and supplication in the Spirit, being watchful to this end with all perseverance and supplication for all of the saints.

EPHESIANS 6:10–18

CHINA CRY

Sarah DeLane has been singing Christian music since she was four. This flagship artist on Bill Gaither's record label performs numerous concerts around the country and twice a year smuggles Bibles into China through the Underground Church. When I asked Sarah how I could get more information about helping the Underground Church in China, she suggested I visit their website at www.hk.super.net/revival.

I interviewed Sarah at my home during one of her visits to Atlanta. I could have listened to her God Stories all day. Here's a sampling:

THE YOUNGEST OF SIX CHILDREN, Sarah DeLane was reared by Christian parents and accepted the Lord as her personal Savior when she was three years old.

Her family was very musical and frequently performed at nursing homes, hospitals, prisons, and churches. Sarah and three of her siblings grew up loving to sing and sharing the gospel whenever and wherever they could.

At the age of seven, Sarah and her family were invited by eighty-year-old missionary Dr. Nora Lamb, whose life story is portrayed in the film *China Cry,* to come overseas and sing as a part of the children's ministries for her crusades.

For four consecutive years, Sarah and her family went to China and ministered in both the adult and the children's crusades in

Taiwan, Korea, the Philippines, and Mainland China. There were audiences of up to 100,000 people.

As she grew older, Sarah's heart continued to long for the opportunity to return to China. She felt it was a part of her heritage and prayed for the chance to go back as an adult and minister to the underground churches.

The atmosphere in China today is quite different from when she was there as a child. Now, the penalty for being caught with religious materials or worshiping God in any way is imprisonment or death. Many churches in that region have stories about how the communist police have persecuted or killed their members for having faith in God.

Sarah details, "On my most recent trip, I came very close to being caught while passing out literature in an apartment building. The communist guards followed my companion and me for many blocks. Eventually, we ducked into a market and bought a soft drink. We were then able to lose the guards by leaving out of a rear exit."

Another such story involves a man Sarah met named Yang. He had been arrested, along with many others, during a raid at one of the underground churches. The communist police took all of their Bibles and confiscated all of their pamphlets. Many members were beaten and a few were killed.

"The communist police hauled Yang and the others to jail. The police singled out Yang and began to interrogate him. They sat him in a chair and told him that if he did not reveal the names of everyone else who had fled the building and then denounce his faith in Jesus Christ, he would be thrown in a dungeon and left there to starve.

"Yang began to cry, but refused to comply with their threats. He told them that he couldn't deny Jesus because He was the One who had given him life. They screamed at him and repeated their threats."

Finally, after hours of trying to get him to talk, they gave up and threw Yang in a dark, damp dungeon.

One might think that after being thrown into such a place of desolation, Yang would have immediately prayed for help, but that was not what he did. Instead, he lifted both hands and began to praise God.

As he was praising God, he was reminded of a Bible story that he had been taught only days before. It was the story of Elijah, which goes like this:

> Elijah was instructed by God to tell the prophets of Baal that there was going to be a drought in the land. God instructed Elijah to go and hide by Cherith Brook so that he would have water and God provided food for him by sending a raven with bread and meat every morning and every night.
>
> Then, when the brook dried up, God sent Elijah to a village called Zarephath and instructed him that there would be a widow there who would feed him.
>
> So he went to Zaraphath. As he arrived at the gates in the city he saw a widow gathering sticks and he asked her for a cup of water. As she was going to get it he called to her and said, "Bring me a piece of bread too."
>
> But she said, "I swear by the Lord your God that I haven't a single piece of bread in the house. And I have only a handful of flour left and a little cooking oil in the bottom of the jar. I was just gathering sticks to cook this last meal, and then my son and I must die of starvation."
>
> But Elijah said to her, "Don't be afraid! Go ahead and cook that last meal but bake me a little loaf of bread first; and afterwards there will still be enough food for you and your son. For the Lord God of Israel says that there will always be plenty of flour and oil left in your containers until the time when the Lord sends rain and the crops grow again."
>
> So she did as Elijah said and she and her son and Elijah continued to eat from her supply of flour and oil as long as it was needed. For no matter how much they used, there was always plenty left in the containers, just as the Lord had promised. (1 Kings 17:1–16)

Sarah goes on, "Yang was extremely encouraged as he remembered the story of Elijah. God had always made whatever provision was necessary to supply the needs of his people."

Yang thought to himself, "So, is God going send a raven with food?"

He opened his eyes and realized how dark it was. He looked up and saw there were no windows anywhere for a raven to fly through. His heart sank.

"Just at that moment, he noticed something out of the corner of his eye. It was a rat! And not just any rat. This rat had an apple in its mouth. He took the apple and ate it.

"The next day, the rat brought him a banana. The following day, the rat brought more fruit. The rat continued to feed Yang for several weeks, totally sustaining his life throughout his prison sentence.

"After some time, the communist guards came, expecting to retrieve and discard the carcass of Yang's dead body. However, when they came, Yang was not only alive, he looked better than when they had jailed him." His condition so disturbed and frightened them that they released him.

"God is the same yesterday, today, and forever. What He did for Elijah, He also did for Yang. In Yang's time of trouble, God fed him from the enemy's table to reward him for his faithfulness. God is always ready and willing to help His children."

❈ ❈ ❈

But without faith it is impossible to please Him, for he who comes to God must believe that He is, and that He is the rewarder of those who diligently seek Him.

HEBREWS 11:6

THE POWER OF PRAYER

Perhaps best known in connection with her husband, Waylon Jennings, Jessi Colter is one of the most significant female singer/songwriters to emerge from the mid-seventies "outlaw" movement. As a singer, Jessi has had a number of successful albums to her credit and in 1975, her composition "I'm Not Lisa" went to #1 on the Billboard charts. As a songwriter, some of the people to record her songs include Nancy Sinatra, Dottie West, and Don Gibson.

I phoned Jessi at their home in Arizona. I had heard a lot about her from her stepson, Terry, and daughter-in-law, Debbie, whom I know from working together in the music business. Jessi was pleasant and peaceful and I enjoyed hearing her story. Debbie had informed me that Jessi is a mighty prayer warrior and can call down all of heaven in one fell swoop. After speaking with her I would have to say that I believe Debbie's assessment is accurate.

❀ ❀ ❀

SUCCESS, UNFORTUNATELY, WAS NOT SOMETHING that came easily to Jessi.

In fact, her life has come full circle. Raised by a Pentecostal mother/minister, Jessi left her roots in search of a more intellectual, metaphysical path. She had been on her search for ten years when she made the decision to return to a personal relationship with the true and living God.

One of the first great supernatural wonders of her life happened in 1975, just as she was launching her solo career in Santa Monica, California. She was singing to the largest crowd for which she had ever performed. But just before the show, she began experiencing an overwhelming sense of fear, unlike anything she had ever known before: "I immediately began calling up all the old tricks I knew to 'center' myself, but nothing worked. As many times as I had performed as a featured artist, fear was gripping me to the point of feeling almost paralyzed.

"At that point, and having just recently returned to my faith in the Lord, I knelt and began to pray. As I did, powerful passages of truth began to rise up in my heart and mind. 'Great peace have those who love Your law, and nothing causes them to stumble.' (Psalm 119:165); I can do all things through Christ who strengthens me (Philippians 4:13); 'Peace I leave with you, My peace I give you; not as the world gives do I give to you. Let not your heart be troubled, neither let it be afraid.' (John 14:27); 'For God has not given us a spirit of fear, but of power and of love and of a sound mind.' (2 Timothy 1:7)

"I began to feel the supernatural power of God rising up on the inside. The more I called on the Lord to give me courage and to help me be strong, the more peaceful I became. I realized that if my trust and confidence was in the Lord and not in my own abilities, everything was going to be fine."

Unknown to her, Jessi's parents who were miles and miles away, had an urging from God that Jessi was fearful and in need of supernatural intervention to bring about a spirit of calmness in her.

"Throughout the show, I had the most exquisite feeling of calm assurance. No drug, no emotional bonding, no psychological attitude or metaphysical deployment could bring about what God can do just by answering the prayers of His children.

"My prayers, along with prayers of my parents, placed me in a moment of time that was elevated above any earthly or human emotion. There is nothing in this world that can put you in that frame of mind. Only God can intervene to bring about such peace."

She praised God for his faithfulness.

It was much later that Jessi learned that her parents had joined hands and prayed for her at precisely the same time she had knelt, calling out to God.

"God loves to hear from us. He invites us to come boldly before the throne at any time and at any place, telling Him what is in our hearts. He desires to give generously to us what we ask of Him.

"When we call on God, He will move mountains, part the Red Sea, turn water to wine—whatever it takes to usher us into a position where we are bathed in His omnipotent power, His unpenetrable protection, and His peace that passes all understanding."

Have I not commanded you? Be strong and of good courage; do not be afraid, not be dismayed, for the LORD your God is with you wherever you go.

JOSHUA 1:9

It's a Beautiful Day
in the Neighborhood

I T SEEMED TO BE THE MIDDLE OF THE NIGHT when the alarm
went off. I didn't mind, though, because God had provided
an incredible opportunity for me. I was getting to meet with
Celia Froehlig, the president of EMI Publishing, to discuss the
possibility of a publishing deal for my country music catalog.

My attorney had described Celia as one of the two most powerful women in Nashville. When he asked me how I had managed to get the appointment, I told him I had called her, asked
her to meet with me, she said yes, and I was on my way. This
meeting was definitely an act of God's favor and I was anxious
to get to speak with her.

At 8:45 A.M., it was already a sweltering 98 degrees in down-
town Nashville. Since my meeting wasn't until 9:30 A.M. I decided to stop in the Nashville Bagel Shop for a little breakfast.
There were no parking spaces available, so I parked next door at
Captain D's. Since Captain D's didn't open until 11 A.M., I thought
there'd be no problem.

I ran in to the bagel shop. There were about six people in line
ahead of me. My turn came and I ordered an egg bagel and coffee to go. I got my order, paid for it, and was out the door just in
time to see my car already up on a flatbed tow truck, being pulled
out onto the street. I ran, yelling at the driver, but he quickly
disappeared out of sight.

There I was, with an incredibly important appointment and
no way to get there. I had taken only a $5 bill out of my wallet

for breakfast. I couldn't call a cab because my briefcase, currently in my backseat with my wallet in it, had also been towed. What a beautiful day in the neighborhood!

I began walking to my appointment, about three miles away. In a business suit, dress shoes, and with the temperature hovering at around 100 degrees, three miles seemed like a walk across the Mojave Desert.

I arrived, soaking wet, with huge blisters on my heels and limp hair plastered to my head. It was not a pretty sight. I apologized for being late. Thankfully, I had sent a tape of some of my songs to Celia prior to our meeting.

Celia greeted me warmly and offered me something cold to drink. When I relayed to Celia the events of the morning, she laughed heartily.

She was very complimentary about my writing and asked me to send her more of my material. She said she would have the whole staff listen to it and see if they thought I was worth signing. I was excited.

After my meeting, I called my friend Maggie to bring money and pick me up. I got my car back and headed home to Atlanta.

Several weeks later, Celia called to say that everyone had liked my material, but they didn't think I brought anything to the table that they didn't already have. Down, but not out, I continued to pursue a publishing deal over the next year, meeting with everyone I could. I was determined not to give up.

Everyone turned me down.

I didn't get it. I had over two hundred recorded songs to my writing credit. Many of my songs had charted to the Top 5 on the radio. If I could have this kind of success in Gospel/ Contemporary Christian music, I knew I could do it in country music, too, if someone would just believe in me and take a chance.

Eventually I returned to Nashville. I had just dropped off a tape at Starstruck Publishing, Reba McEntire's company, and was calling my next appointment from the car. There was a tap on my window —my friend Jason Houser. I found out later that he was starting a new job the following Monday at, of all places, EMI. I told him I had met at EMI with Celia Froehlig the year before. Jason informed me that Celia was no longer with EMI, but had started her own company. He jotted down her name and a new number for me.

Later, I phoned Celia, reminded her of who I was, and congratulated her on the new venture. I asked if I could stop by sometime and play her some more tunes. She told me to come on by the next time I was up.

Not long after that, I met with Celia and her partner, Robin Palmer. I took them twenty new songs. After a month or so, they called to say they loved two of them and would like to begin pitching them. Within two weeks, "The Hard Way," which I cowrote with my friend Keith Brown, had been put on hold for multi-platinum artist Faith Hill. I was ecstatic, but they warned me this could be a long, drawn-out process.

They weren't kidding.

"The Hard Way" was on hold for a year. We were told that Faith had listened to thousands of songs. She recorded thirty-six of those songs, and then finally narrowed it down to the twelve that would make the record. "The Hard Way" was one of the twelve. Finally, I had my first country cut!

On June 23, 1998, I received my first platinum album commemorating one million sales of Faith Hill's record with my song on it. On May 25, 1999, at a beautiful ceremony in Nashville, Faith Hill herself presented Keith, Celia, Robin, and me with our own triple platinum record.

Thankfully, things don't always end up the way they originally start out. Today, it is indeed, a beautiful day in the neighborhood!

❀ ❀ ❀

This Book of the Law shall not depart from your mouth, but you shall meditate in it day and night that you may observe to do according to all that is written in it. For then you will make your way prosperous and then you will have good success.

JOSHUA 1:8

Everybody's Somebody

Ollie E. Brown began his career as a musician touring with such notable artists as Stevie Wonder and the Rolling Stones. He also played on the CDs of Michael Jackson, The Jacksons, Barbra Streisand, Diana Ross, and Quincy Jones.

Currently, he's the Senior Vice President and General Manager of Click Records, a division of Dick Clark Productions. The label is devoted to "old school" acts. New CDs by The 5th Dimension and The Spinners are forthcoming.

I met Ollie through our mutual friend, Zoro the drummer, and interviewed him by phone from Los Angeles as he huffed and puffed on his Stairmaster. I enjoyed meeting him and hope to see him on my next trip to Los Angeles.

Having traveled all over the world, Ollie has had the opportunity to view life from many different perspectives. From the most affluent to the poorest of the poor, Ollie E. Brown has seen it all.

He has often contemplated why some people seem to have so much and others have little or nothing at all. Because he had been so blessed with financial prosperity, he was always willing to write a check to help someone in need.

❀ ❀ ❀

S TANDING ON THE STREET CORNER outside of his church, Ollie had seen the same homeless person holding the same sign for weeks on end. As the man extended an empty hat to passersby or cars stopped in traffic, Ollie had frequently contributed a few dollars.

"One day, I felt the Lord prompting me to stop and talk with the man. The first thing I learned was that the man had a name. It was Brad. Brad had lost his job, his home, and his family and truly wanted help in trying to put his life back together."

So Ollie invited Brad to come inside the church and suggested that he also consider becoming a member. Ollie explained to Brad that he would more likely get the help he was looking for if he began developing relationships. If they got the chance to know Brad, the members of the church would be more willing to provide the tools he needed to turn things around.

Brad agreed and Ollie introduced him to the assistant pastor. Immediately Brad was hired on the spot to do odd jobs around the church.

Ollie established that Brad was sincere and committed to doing a good job by always being dependable. One day, Ollie felt the Lord prompting him to assist Brad in getting an apartment by paying his rent for several months.

"After I helped him get into an apartment, Brad stopped coming to church for a while. I was about to check up on him when Brad showed up with the good news that he had secured a new job and had been reunited with his family, all in the apartment that God prompted me to facilitate. The opportunity for Brad to put his life back in order began with God instructing me to embrace Ollie's physical, emotional, spiritual and financial needs, rather than simply writing a check."

It was nearing Christmas and Ollie had been very moved by the results of his personal involvement with Brad. He decided to get involved in the Feed the Hungry campaign over the holidays and informed all of his friends that they would not be receiving gifts from him that year. Instead, he was spending his gift budget on helping those in need.

Ollie's pastor considered all of the members of the church to be ministers, so he didn't just collect money, then buy and deliver the food. He had those in need submit their names and requests, which were then compiled into a master list. This way, the church members who felt led to become involved in providing food for those in need could approach people directly.

When Ollie contacted the family he had been assigned, rather than buying things without knowing what they needed, he decided to take the family along with him. That way they could pick out exactly what they needed.

"I arrived at their house and told them my plan," Ollie said. "We all got into my car, went to the grocery store, and bought everything they needed. When we returned home, I noticed that their refrigerator was so small that the groceries would barely fit.

"The family had two small children. One was a little girl about the same age as one of my children. I had noticed throughout the shopping spree, again on their ride home, and even as they were unpacking the groceries that this little girl continually smiled at me. I was humbled to realize that this little girl was as happy just to have food on the table as my children were about having their Christmas tree packed with presents."

Ollie couldn't bear the thought of these children not having any gifts for Christmas, so he insisted on taking them to a toy store. He told the children they could get whatever they desired. He wanted to make something they had dreamed about come true.

What happened next surprised Ollie. Each of the children picked out only one gift. The little girl picked out a doll and the little boy picked out a guitar. Ollie couldn't believe how excited the children were over receiving one toy.

"Looking into the faces of people you've just met and allowing God to use you to meet their needs results in a natural high that is indescribable. It benefits the giver as much or more than it does the recipient.

"Occasionally, we can become apathetic and lazy about attending church. We feel content to pray and worship God from home and think we don't really need to be a part of a congregation. If I had stayed home the Sunday I met Brad, not only would Brad have missed out on meeting someone who helped him change his situation, but I would have missed out on getting a blessing, as well.

"If I had stayed home on the Sunday when the pastor solicited volunteers to feed the hungry, I might never have known about it and another blessing could have been missed.

"It's much easier to write a check than to get personally involved with homelessness and poverty. But getting personally involved has forever changed me."

❁ ❁ ❁

"I was hungry and you gave Me food, I was thirsty and you gave me drink; I was a stranger and you took Me in; I was naked and you clothed Me; I was sick and you visited Me; I was in prison and you came to Me."

Then the righteous will answer Him saying, "Lord, when did we . . . feed You or . . . give You a drink? When did we take You in or clothe you? When were You sick and we visited You or in prison and we came to You?"

And Jesus will answer them saying, "Inasmuch as you did it to one of the least of these you did it unto Me."

MATTHEW 25:35–40

AN AUDIENCE
WITH THE KING

Dolly Parton says, "There are really only three female singers
in the world: Streisand, Ronstadt, and Connie Smith. The rest
of us are only pretending." With over fifty albums released and
forty-eight Billboard chart singles, Connie Smith was inducted
as an Opry member in 1965. Several of the songs on her current
self-titled release were cowritten with her husband Marty Stuart.
Connie supports YWAM (Youth With a Mission) and Daystar,
a counseling service in Nashville, Tennessee.

I spoke with Connie by phone from Nashville and we faxed
back and forth a few more times until her story was exactly as
she wanted it. I loved her tender heart and her desire that her
story be used of God to touch lives.

❀ ❀ ❀

BEING FROM A LARGE FAMILY who was extremely poor, and
having a father who was an alcoholic, Connie Smith grew
up feeling that no one loved her. After her parents divorced, her
mother later married a man with eight children. They had one
child together and, along with her five, they became a blended
family with fourteen children.

The older children in the family needed supervision so they
would stay in line and out of trouble. The younger kids had to
be watched so that they could be protected from getting hurt.
Connie was right in the middle, so she watched everybody.

Connie, along with all of her siblings, tried to get her own needs met. Having only one mother to meet those needs, Connie quickly developed people-pleaser skills and tried to extract the love and nurturing every child so desperately needs.

"When we had company, I would be the child who would offer the guest a chair or a glass of water. I felt that doing good deeds and trying to be perfect was the only way anyone would notice me or acknowledge my existence. "If anyone extended warmth or affection toward me, however, I would put up an inner wall. I thought if anyone knew me like I knew myself, there would be no way they would like me."

Connie continued struggling with her lack of self-worth. The more she attempted to do everything right, the worse even the smallest failure would make her feel about herself.

Connie's family never went to church, but occasionally she'd go to church with a stepcousin who had given Connie a Bible.

Connie had spent so much of her life trying to get approval and wanting to be accepted by everyone, that it was impossible for her to believe that the Holy God of the entire universe loved her no matter what.

When she first moved to Nashville, as is the case with a lot of people who were reared in poverty, Connie was very proud and tried to keep her past a secret in order to protect herself: "I'd not been to church in a long time and one Sunday was invited to go. As I sat in the service and the pastor spoke of the tender, caring love of God through Jesus Christ, I began to weep. I was embarrassed that those around me were seeing me cry. Over the years, I had learned to protect myself by hiding my real feelings. Once again, I stopped going to church.

"One day, a pastor knocked on my front door. When I answered the door, he began telling me about Jesus. I felt that he had invaded my privacy and was very rude to him. I was quick to let him know that he wasn't welcome."

Some time later, Connie was invited to sing on Jimmy Roger Snow's Television Easter Special. She was comfortable with the format because, after all, she did believe in God and loved hymns.

"While taping the program, the Easter story was shared. To my amazement I cried, just as I had in church. Jimmy noticed my tears and immediately recognized the spirit of God dealing with my heart. After the show, he took me aside, opened his Bible, and explained the plan of salvation to me."

Jimmy read scripture to Connie and told her, "Sin separated us from God and the penalty for our sins is death and hell. God loves us, but because He is holy and just, sin cannot enter into His presence. God had to come up with a means through which our sins could be paid for, but that provision had to be made by someone who was acceptable to Him and sinless."

He continued by reading more scripture and then said, "If there had been only YOU, God would still have sent Jesus to take your place on the cross to pay for your sins. You would be totally forgiven, fully accepted by God, and, once again, reconciled to Him forever."

Connie started going to Jimmy's church. Almost every week, she would go down to the front during the altar call, because she still had feelings of unworthiness.

One evening during a revival at her church, the visiting evangelists, Doyne and Gladness Jennings, asked if there was anyone there who had received the gift of salvation, but would like to be filled with the power of the Holy Spirit. Connie went forward.

Two ladies began to pray for her loudly and simultaneously. This was new to Connie. She became distracted and irritated, couldn't concentrate, and in an effort to drown them out, Connie began to say aloud, "Thank you, Jesus! Thank you, Jesus!"

Suddenly the joy and the peace of the Lord began to flow through Connie and she felt the love of God like never before. Immediately, that old feeling that nobody loved her welled up inside.

"Just as quickly, I recalled the scripture that says God knows our hearts better than we do. For the first time in my life, I real-

ized that, in spite of all my shortcomings, God loved me uncon-
ditionally.

"All of a sudden, a knowledge came from deep within. I realized that God wasn't just out there on a pedestal, but that He
could actually be part of my life. I remembered thinking, "I have
an audience with the King!

"I finally realized that the fullness of my salvation included
peace, joy, contentment, power, protection, mercy, grace, *and*
love. All of that belongs to me because I belong to God."

[We are] accepted in the Beloved. In Him we have re-
demption through His blood, the forgiveness of sins,
according to the riches of His grace which He made to
abound toward us in all wisdom and prudence.

EPHESIANS 1:6–8

184

BUY A WHAT?

I WALKED OUT OF MY AIR-CONDITIONED CONDO into what felt like an outdoor steam room. It was officially the first day of summer, although the hot and sultry temperatures we'd been experiencing for the last three weeks made it feel like summer had arrived long before.

I was headed to several appointments and decided to make my way by secondary roads, rather than by the expressway. As I was silently collecting my thoughts and reviewing the objectives for my first appointment, a command shot through my mind: "Go buy a swimsuit."

I responded aloud. "Go buy a *what?*"

I was stunned by such a thought because I hadn't worn a swimsuit in years. I was much too overweight and self-conscious to even consider such an idea. I tried to ignore it, but once again, the thought shot through my mind, this time louder: "Go buy a swimsuit!"

I wasn't sure why God wanted me to have a swimsuit, but I was sure that this was His idea and definitely not mine. I pulled into the Target parking lot, parked, and went in. I tried on a few swimsuits, found one that fit, purchased it, and went on my way.

Following my appointments, I headed back home. As I drove, I noticed the Target bag on the front seat and began to think again about the odd instruction to buy a swimsuit. I mean, in the twelve years since I had owned my condo, I had only been to the pool one time.

Having been born in Miami and reared in Fort Lauderdale, I always loved the water and enjoyed swimming. So, I began telling myself that having the extra weight was just the way I was and it was nothing to be ashamed of. I became convinced that God wanted me to enjoy my summer, including the refreshing, invigorating joy of an occasional dip in the pool. I just figured that must have been why He put it in my heart to get a swimsuit.

As soon as I arrived home, I put on my new swimsuit and headed for the pool. I swam a few laps and then settled into a lounge chair to read a while. As I baked to medium-well, I decided I needed to take another dip to cool off. About that time, two women in their late fifties came through the gate with a small boy about five years old. The women carried a cooler, some towels, and a bottle of suntan lotion. The boy had an unopened diver's mask and a gigantic squirt gun.

I swam a few more laps and the boy began to open his new toys. Seated on the steps, he put on the mask and began to fill up his squirt gun.

After my last lap, I joined him on the steps. We said hello and then I turned my head away from him, looking around at the trees, flowers, and shrubs that surrounded the pool area.

I made a mental note that the next time I saw the groundskeepers, I would thank them for doing such a great job around the property. I was so happy and content to enjoy the beautiful day and felt blessed to be able to enjoy it poolside.

When I looked back where the little boy had been sitting, I noticed that he was no longer there. He had pushed himself off the steps and was now a few feet away from me. He was totally submerged underwater. His mask was covering his face, but I could see an expression of panic, which let me know that he probably couldn't swim and was in trouble. I lunged forward, picked him up out of the water and pulled off his mask. Due to swallowing several big gulps of chlorinated water, he choked and gasped for air. I held him tight and assured him I wouldn't let him drop. He shivered and cried in short, quiet little whimpers.

The women with whom he had come were busy chatting and

enjoying their cold drinks. Neither had noticed the little boy struggling or that he had been only seconds away from drowning.

One of the women, his grandmother, finally looked over and inquired about the ruckus. I relayed what had happened and informed them that the child could not swim. I suggested they might consider watching him a little more closely, gave the boy a hug, and then decided to be on my way.

Back in my condo as I pulled off my wet suit, I remembered what had seemed to be such an unusual thought some seven hours earlier: "Go buy a swimsuit!"

I know there are probably many times when God attempts to direct our paths and we fail to hear Him. Or maybe we just fail to comply. This time I was really glad I had gone along with the program, even though it didn't make sense, nor was it something on my personal agenda. For once, I didn't try to figure things out; I just obeyed, knowing that the thought was not my own. For whatever reason God wanted me to have a swimsuit and, at least for a time, I got to know why.

As I remember holding that precious little boy in my arms and looking into his eyes as the fear melted away, I'm glad that God spoke to me that morning. I'm even more grateful that I listened.

❀ ❀ ❀

Trust in the LORD with all of your heart and lean not on your own understanding. In all your ways acknowledge Him and He will direct your path.

PROVERBS 3:5–6

GOD'S PLANS ARE BIG!

I interviewed Greg Nelson, the award-winning producer and songwriter, up close and personal at Starstruck, Reba McEntire's recording studio in Nashville, Tennessee, where he was producing another of his excellent works.

❀ ❀ ❀

FOR THE LAST FOUR OR FIVE YEARS, Greg Nelson has had a dream. That dream is to see the book *Pilgrim's Progress*, one of his favorite pieces of literature, adapted into a screenplay and released as a feature film.

Paul Bunyun wrote *Pilgrim's Progress* while in prison. It's an allegory that presents an acute interpretation of the Bible, as portrayed through one man's life journey.

Greg and his partner, Bob Farrell, had spent endless hours brainstorming about the possibilities of developing such a project. They had written several pieces of music for it and discussed whether the best way to present their vision was as a musical, an animated film, or as a live action film.

After putting their presentation package together, they had several meetings with production entities. Nothing ever came of the meetings and after several rejections with potential co-venture partners, Greg decided to let the idea go.

In the meantime, John, a very wealthy Christian man, contacted Greg. John lives in a castle in Europe and was familiar with Greg's work as a record producer. He wanted to meet with Greg to discuss the possibility of producing a special record project for the millennium.

"I flew to Europe, where I was picked up by a chauffeur and driven to an exclusive hotel. Shortly after being taken to my room, there was a knock on the door. I answered it to find a butler standing there. This butler had been personally assigned to me and had arrived with chilled champagne, an assortment of vintage wines, and a selection of hors d'oeuvres."

Greg, who doesn't drink alcohol and who wasn't hungry, was stunned. The butler informed him that he was there to unpack his luggage and to provide any other services to make Greg's visit more pleasurable. Greg explained to the butler that he, too, was just a working man and didn't really require all the attention.

"Yes," the butler politely offered, "on a few rare occasions, I've been assigned to others of your type."

Still, the butler insisted he needed to unpack for Greg. Greg finally conceded, but warned the manservant that he only had one suit and the only other things he brought were jeans and a few shirts.

"I'll hang them all neatly," the butler replied.

Later that evening, Greg was escorted to the hotel's five-star restaurant, where he dined on seven courses. He then returned to his room and found his bed turned down with Godiva chocolates on his pillow. Greg rested well and awakened the next morning feeling refreshed and in great anticipation of his upcoming appointment.

Following a selection of breakfast foods served on sterling silver platters, Greg was whisked off in a chauffeur-driven limousine to meet John.

"The castle was breathtaking!" Greg explains. "As we turned into the driveway, grounds that looked like a picture-perfect postcard surrounded us. John greeted me and then offered to give me the guided tour, after which we would get down to the business at hand.

"After we began to chat about the record project for the millennium, John asked me about my other interests. I explained to John that I liked to write oratorios and extended choral works for orchestra and soloists.

189

"I also relayed that I was interested in developing a film from the book *Pilgrim's Progress*, because it was a story that I felt needed to be told on film."

Also a fan of *Pilgrim's Progress*, John became thoughtful and began asking Greg questions. He wanted to know about the proposed budget for the film and the plans for distribution. Greg said the project would cost around $40 million and described his ideas for distribution.

It was a productive first meeting. John hired Greg to produce the millennium project and they parted ways. Then Greg checked out of his hotel, was escorted to the airport, and flew back to the United States.

Two days after Greg returned home, John called him, wanting to talk in more detail about the budget needed for *Pilgrim's Progress*.

"Is $40 million the amount of money you need?" John asked, wanting to confirm the exact amount.

"That's correct," said Greg.

"When do you need to have the money?" John continued.

Having been turned down so many times, Greg was unaccustomed to being asked such a pointed question.

"Well, I would like to have the money, or at least access to it, by the end of the year. Then we would be able to begin the development process."

John told Greg he would call him within ten days.

Eight days later, John phoned.

"Greg, about this *Pilgrim's Progress*. We now have the funding for it."

"What?" Greg responded in amazement.

"Yes. I have put up a certain amount of the funding and I have brought in others who will contribute the rest. We've met and decided to fund your project. So, what do we do?"

Greg was overwhelmed. He realized that he hadn't had to do any huge presentation to enact John's involvement. In fact, discussing *Pilgrim's Progress* had only been a small part of their conversation.

Greg is sure it was God who had prepared John's heart. Greg believes, "Undeniably, John had been primed and prompted for involvement in *Pilgrim's Progress* long before I ever brought up the subject. God faithfully provided exactly what was needed to bring God's vision to fruition.

"Getting a $40 million film funded in less than two weeks would normally be impossible! The more we get to know God, however, the more we understand that nothing is too hard for Him."

*Ah, L*ORD *God! Behold, You have made the heavens and the earth by Your great power and outstretched arm. There is nothing too hard for You.*

JEREMIAH 32:17

OUT OF THE
MOUTHS OF BABES

As a free agent, Joe Jacoby was signed as an offensive lineman with the Washington Redskins in 1981 where he continued to play for thirteen years. He played in four Super Bowls and won three of them. He also played in four Pro Bowls. In 1998, he was nominated for the Hall of Fame, and in 1999, Joe was inducted into the Washington Hall of Stars. He is active in the Joe Gibbs Youth Homes for at-risk and troubled youth.

I met Joe through my friend Jennifer Kemp Andrews and found him to be delightful.

※ ※ ※

NFL GREAT, JOE JACOBY hadn't missed too many Kentucky Derby's. He was, after all, born and raised in Louisville, Kentucky.

Even after thirteen years as a linebacker for the Washington Redskins, and after getting married and moving to Virginia, Joe always made every effort possible to return home and attend the event that had become internationally known as the centerpiece for his home state.

"I knew about God and had attended church for most of my life," Joe explains, "but throughout my years in pro sports, I didn't often participate in matters related to spiritual things. I enjoyed all the perks that came with being a football hero and preferred partying and having fun over having fellowship with God and His saints."

After marrying Irene and moving to Virginia, Joe left football and went into business for himself. Soon after having their first child, Lauren, Joe began thinking about his responsibility to teach his daughter about God. She was smart enough to know and love Barney, but up until this point, there had been no discussions or references in their home to God.

Joe became convicted about the importance of bringing up his daughter with a knowledge and awareness of God. So the young family began the process of visiting different congregations to find a church home.

May rolled around and, along with an old college buddy, Joe jetted off to the Kentucky Derby.

Meanwhile, on a beautiful Sunday morning back in Virginia, Irene and Lauren were preparing to go to church. Irene, who was pregnant with their second child, put the family dog outside in the gated backyard. Lauren wanted to go outside and play with her pal until it was time to leave for church, so Irene consented, as she finished the breakfast dishes.

The dog had recently undergone hip replacement surgery, and when the dog was petted in that sensitive area, this normally mild-mannered animal became ferocious.

Suddenly, Irene heard a ruckus in the backyard. As she looked out the window, all she could see was the dog viciously attacking Lauren. Irene ran out the back door and pulled the dog off of Lauren. Her face was covered in blood and she was going in and out of consciousness.

Instinctively, Irene wrapped Lauren in a blanket, ran her to the van, strapped Lauren into her carseat, and headed to the local fire department.

Five minutes later, as she arrived at the fire station, Irene jumped from her car almost before it had fully come to a halt. As she attempted to explain to the firemen what had happened, they began to scold her for bringing Lauren into town rather than calling 911.

Irene insisted that they were wasting valuable time and that Lauren didn't have time to hear a lecture. She opened the side of the van to reveal Lauren in the backseat. As soon as the firemen realized Lauren's condition, they immediately escorted them to the nearest emergency room.

Lauren had multiple lacerations to her face and head. Her nose was almost completely detached and she had lost an enormous amount of blood. They immediately took her into surgery and Irene began praying. A nurse tried to track down Joe at the Derby.

When the phone rang in his hotel room, Joe was horrified to be contacted by a nurse whose first words were that, although his little girl was in surgery, she was going to be "all right." All he could think about was that he had to get home so that he could be there when she came out of surgery.

"Unfortunately, it was the day after the Derby. Everyone was leaving Louisville, and there were no seats on any of the flights. I prayed about what to do and asked God to do something so I could get back to my little girl. I did the only thing I knew to do. I chartered a small plane.

"During the flight back, the weather was turbulent. The plane was flying in between clusters of violent thunderstorms, and the plane was tossed about like a toy. My friend from college became airsick and I just prayed we would arrive safely and that I would make it to the hospital."

When they finally landed at national airport in Washington, D.C., Joe caught a cab and left his friend to claim their luggage and retrieve his car.

"As I walked into the hospital, Lauren was coming out of recovery. She had over two hundred stitches on her nose. Part of her lip and the corner of her eye also required extensive plastic surgery. The surgeon told Irene and me that because of her age and losing so much blood, she came close to dying. But God was watching over her and had intervened, sparing her life. God gave Lauren back to us."

Seeing his baby on a gurney with her head and face totally bandaged brought Joe to tears. Joe and Irene bent over her and let Lauren know they were there with her.

Lauren looked up at both of her parents and said in her soft little voice, "God sent me back to you."

Those words changed their lives and will always be something they cherish. Since that day, Irene and Joe have been committed Christians.

Lauren is now ten years old and is one of the top swimmers in the state of Virginia. She has great love for her younger sister, Jenna, and a passion for dogs. Especially the two who now live at their house.

She also loves God and knows how much He loves and cares for her. Valuable truths can come from the mouths of babes. That day, Joe and Irene learned a truth they will never forget.

❀ ❀ ❀

Train up a child in the way he should go, and when he is old he will not depart from it.

PROVERBS 22:6

THE ANDRE CROUCH
CONNECTION

FOR THE ENTIRE FIRST YEAR AFTER BECOMING a Christian, I had not written even one song. In fact I couldn't even seem to make two words rhyme.

Prior to that, I could remember nights when I sat at the piano and wrote six or seven tunes in one sitting. The morning after, I'd always review my work to see if it was as great as I'd remembered or if my opinion had been as much under the influence as I had been. Oddly enough, in most instances, the songs were strong and well-crafted.

That was when I was a party girl. But since then, I'd laid down the scotch and all the other party favors. I concluded that my songwriting talents had been drug-related, and because I no longer got high and my party days were over, I assumed my ability to craft songs was now buried.

One Saturday afternoon, I ran through a bookstore to buy a book. As I was driving away, my head suddenly began to fill with music and lyrics. I was stunned. This had not occurred for so long and I had become convinced that this moment would never happen again. But it was definitely happening and I didn't want to miss it.

I quickly pulled back into a parking space and searched for something to write with. Anything would do—a pen, a pencil, lipstick, fingernail polish, eyeliner. I found an eyebrow pencil. Now, I just needed something to write on. The book I had purchased was in a paper bag. The paper bag would do just fine.

Then the most wonderful thing happened. I wrote one song

on the front of the bag and another on the back. I put my car in reverse and backed out of the parking space. My tears made it difficult to see. As I drove home, I quietly praised the Lord for the gift He'd just given me. I realized how much I had missed writing. Some friends of mine from my singles class at church had loaned me some Christian records. The one I liked best was by Andre Crouch. He had written classics like "To God Be The Glory," "Through It All," "I Have Confidence," and "The Blood." His music was inspiring, powerful, and anointed. So when I got inside my apartment, I put on Andre's record. It was beginning to dawn on me that God wanted me to use my songwriting talents in a new area. There had been many occasions when I had abused His gift. But it was clear to me now that God wanted me to write songs for and about Him.

As I prayed, I said, "Okay, God, I'll write songs for you, but if I do this, I'd really like to be good at it. I want to write like Andre Crouch."

Thankfully, God understood what I meant and loved me right where I was.

The next day at church, my music minister, Joe Estes, sang a solo just before the sermon. Most of the time, Joe would have done a song written by Bill Gaither, but today was different. As the introduction to the music began, I recognized the piece to be a medley of Andre Crouch songs.

Well, the floodgates opened and I began to weep profusely. I drank in the music. It was as though the God of the universe had taken my face in His hands and was intimately, positively confirming my request from the day before.

Some time later, I was in Nashville completing production on a record. I planned to drive home that evening before heading to Los Angeles, but just as I was about to leave, I got a call from a friend of mine. She said she wanted me to come to California a day early so that I could go to a birthday party with her. She refused to tell me whose party, but strongly suggested I try and work it out.

I decided to go for it.

My friend picked me up at the airport and we headed to the birthday party. I still had not figured out where we were going. We pulled up to a beautiful home with cars lining the streets. As we entered the house, a lot of friendly people began to introduce themselves.

We rounded the corner into the living room and I spotted a long, ebony grand piano. There was a crowd gathered around it, blocking my view of who was sitting on the piano stool. As people around the piano turned to speak to my friend, the occupant of the piano stool was revealed. It was Andre Crouch. This was his home and the birthday party was for him and his twin sister, Sandra. I couldn't believe it.

I was introduced to both of them and later that evening, I stood at the end of the grand piano as Andre sang all the songs that had come to mean so much to me. We exchanged phone numbers.

Andre's dad was a preacher, and on one of my next trips, I went to hear him preach. Before the sermon, a woman about eighty years old took the platform to give her testimony. She talked about Isaiah 51 and how we can learn to soar like eagles. She said when a mother eagle teaches her babies how to fly, she takes them up as high in the air as she can and then drops them. Just before they hit the ground, she flies underneath them and swoops them up onto her wings. She repeats this seven or eight times until the babies are so exhausted, they give up struggling and relax. When they do, the wind lifts their wings and causes them to fly.

The woman's testimony gave me an idea for a song, which I began writing.

After church, Andre and Sandra invited me over for lunch. I told Andre that I had been inspired by the older woman and had jotted down the words to a new song.

He asked to see them.

Andre then went to his piano and asked me to come over and

sit beside him. I did. He began playing a melody to my lyrics. I taped it. I was actually co-writing a song with my idol.

The best part of all was to realize that before the foundation of the earth and before God ever hung the first star, He scheduled my connections with Andre Crouch. He orchestrated them for the sole purpose of doing a new thing in me. And a new thing it was!

❀ ❀ ❀

Do not remember the former things, nor consider the things of old. Behold, I will do a new thing, now it shall spring forth; shall you not know it? I will even make a road in the wilderness and rivers in the desert.

ISAIAH 43:18–19

Okay, God,
I Need A Job . . . Today!

Singer/actress Cynthia Calhoun has sung background vocals and studio sessions with Gloria Estefan, Jon Secada, Barry White, Boz Skaggs, and Steely Dan. She's appeared in television episodes of *The Parenthood, The Wayans Brothers, Where I Live* with Doug E. Doug, *Rhythm and Jam* with Brandy, and *ER*. She's also appeared in several films including *Menace 2 Society* starring Lorenz Tate, Jada Pinkett-Smith, and Charles Dutton.

I interviewed Cynthia from her new home in Orlando, Florida. She is one of the funniest women I know. Each time she leaves a message on my answering service, I'm never sure which of her myriad of characters she will be.

One day she left a message as a militant black woman named Millisha. Another day she was a representative of Critters for Christ because, after all, cows, pigs, and chickens need the Lord, too! I am certain that it's only a matter of time before she has her own sitcom.

NINE MONTHS BEFORE SHE ARRIVED in Los Angeles with stars in her eyes and a life-long dream in her heart, Cynthia Calhoun wanted to *make it*!

She had auditioned for everything from doing cat food commercials to dressing up like a leprechaun and singing birthday telegrams. Even amidst all of her enthusiasm, nothing was working.

Down to her last few dollars, Cynthia bolted out of bed one morning with only one prayer request on her lips: "Okay, God, I know who you are and I don't mean to be pushy, but I need a job . . . today!"

Cynthia's schedule for the day was lined up. She had one audition and had volunteered to drive around several friends who needed transportation. She figured she might as well give herself one last whirl around the city before packing up and moving back home. Carting her friends around would be a way of doing that . . . unless, of course, God managed to get her a job . . . today!

Cynthia completed her audition. Then she headed to pick up her friend Elise Neal from an audition and take her to the airport. As Elise got into the car, she told Cynthia that after dropping her at the airport, she should go back and audition for the job she had just tried out for.

Cynthia thought about it, but told Elise that by the time she made her way back through traffic, the auditions would probably be over. Moreover, she didn't have an appointment to audition, nor did she have an agent who could call and set up an appointment. Elise felt strongly that Cynthia was exactly what they were looking for, however, and made Cynthia promise she'd go back by.

Cynthia never breaks a promise so she headed back to Melrose Drive.

She entered the Raleigh Studios and told the security guard she was there for an audition. He pointed her to the designated waiting area and, as she had anticipated, everyone had already gone. But there was a door inside the room and she knew that there was a chance that the casting director was still on the other side of that door.

Cynthia thought to herself, "Oh well, I did what I said I would do, but everyone's gone so I may as well go home."

But something inside her said, Cynthia, you've come this far, why don't you knock on the door?

"I raised my hand to knock and then froze. Once again, doubts consumed me and I thought I should just leave. But before I could lower my hand, the door opened."

The man she stood eye to eye with smiled at her and said kiddingly, "I felt you!" They both laughed.

The man introduced himself as the casting director and asked if he could help her. Stammering, Cynthia said, "I came for the audition."

"What time was your appointment?" he asked.

"Uh, well, to be honest, I didn't have an appointment. But I just want to audition."

"Who is your agent?" he inquired.

"Uh, actually, I don't have an agent," she said sheepishly.

The casting director told her that he didn't normally do this but he would allow her to audition.

"And you'd better be good!" he said.

She was good and he told her to report back the next day for callbacks.

Cynthia was elated! The casting director told her the part was for a "hoochie" girl. Hailing from Florida and not being completely familiar with the description of the character, she borrowed an outfit from her roommate and returned the next day. She was nicely clad in a very classy ensemble.

The casting director looked at her and said, "What are you doing?"

She responded, "I'm here for the audition."

"How far do you live from here?" he asked.

"About twenty minutes."

"Good. Go home and put on another outfit. You look too nice. You need to be dressed like a 'hoochie' girl—a thug!"

Now that was a term Cynthia understood. All the way home she marveled at the fact that casting directors never let you audition without an appointment or agency representation. And they *certainly* don't tell you what to wear and send you home to get a second chance. Within twenty minutes, Cynthia arrived back at the auditions in short shorts, a halter top, and an overabundance of jewelry—she looked the part.

As she stood before the panel of judges, Cynthia very quietly stated her name. Because of her timidity, she felt they were thinking she had no chance and wanted her to hurry up and get it over with.

But when she opened her mouth to do the part, she became this loud "hoochie mama girl." The judges became wide-eyed and their mouths hung open. They began to laugh and talk among themselves. The judges and the casting director began singing her praises.

Following the audition, she once again regressed and in a quiet, mild manner, thanked them for their time.

Many of the people auditioning were well-known and Cynthia was certain one of them would land the part. But she took great pleasure in knowing that she did a good job and that they had liked her.

A couple of weeks later, Cynthia flew to Miami to sing background vocals for Gloria Estefan and Jon Secada at a fundraiser for a hurricane relief effort in the aftermath of Hurricane Andrew.

"The day after the concert, I checked my voicemail in Los Angeles and picked up a message from the casting director informing me I needed to be at the final callback later that day. I phoned to tell him where I was and asked if there was any way he could see me tomorrow. He said there was no way."

Cynthia was disappointed, but still felt positive about having had the experience. When she got off the phone she began praying, "God, You can intervene supernaturally in this situation and still make it happen, if in fact that's in Your plan. You know I really need a job. I'm asking You to give me favor with these people, even though I can't be there. Amen."

A couple of hours went by and the casting director called Cynthia back. They had finished with the auditions but kept being drawn to review her audition videotape. They had unanimously concluded that Cynthia was the best candidate for the job. She was hired for the part and was cast in the acclaimed feature film *Menace 2 Society*!

"I couldn't believe it! The job allowed me to remain in Los Angeles, where I continued to follow my dreams. The experience also confirmed that God not only hears our prayers but answers them!"

❀ ❀ ❀

Give ear, O LORD, to my prayer. And attend to the voice of my supplications. In the day of my trouble I will call upon You for You will answer me.

PSALM 86:6–7

OCEAN VIEW

I T HAD BEEN A WHIRLWIND WEEK of meetings in Los Angeles, but relief was in sight. My girlfriend Gloria Hawkins, at whose apartment I was staying, convinced me that we needed a break from all the madness. She suggested that we go to Laguna Beach for the weekend.

Gloria reeled off the highlights of Laguna as if she were president of the Chamber of Commerce. She described the quaintness of the small resort. She said we could walk everywhere with the ocean always in sight. We could have a latte while watching the sunset, browse all the shops, take in the art, smell the fresh-cut flowers, and dine on unlimited quantities of fresh seafood. I had never been there before and I was convinced.

We decided to stay at a hotel where Gloria had stayed before. It had a pool, a workout room, a hot tub, and a sauna. (We requested two queen-size beds, and got the last room they had with an ocean view.) (Our room also had its own private balcony overlooking the woods.)

On the ride down, we began to get excited about what was ahead of us. We decided to wait until we arrived to have dinner, so we could begin our holiday with fresh seafood.

We arrived around 8:30 P.M. and checked into our hotel. It was already dark, so as we walked to our room, we realized it would be morning before we could enjoy our ocean view. Without surveying the room too closely, we threw our bags down and headed off on foot, seeking an outdoor cafe that served seafood.

We didn't find an outdoor cafe, but we did find one where we could sit by opened jalousie windows, allowing us to smell the salt air and hear the crashing waves. The shrimp and scallops were succulent. Except for several disruptions by some young people who were screaming at each other outside, we leisurely enjoyed our dinner.

Suddenly, and without warning, another dispute erupted on the street. Just outside our window, hoodlums were spraying each other with mace. Was this the peaceful Laguna we'd been dreaming about? As we turned to observe the ruckus, a huge cloud of acrid fog began to float through our windows and onto us.

As the cloud collided with our eyes, nostrils, and throats, we began gasping for air. The hot-peppered aerosol caused us to cough uncontrollably. Soon we were in the ladies room, giving up the delightful dinner we had just consumed, in a most undelightful way.

We had just been "maced" in the quiet little beachside community of Laguna! We could have had this wonderful experience without ever leaving Los Angeles. We left and went to Starbuck's to regroup and enjoy a latte.

As we unpacked our clothes, we noticed several things—the bathroom door didn't close all the way, we were missing the "hot" knob on our shower, and our mattresses and pillows were worn and lumpy. We had no towels and only one washcloth. Soap was nowhere to be found.

"I'll call the front desk and give them our list of grievances," Gloria announced.

"Good," I responded. "I'm going to go out on the balcony and drink my latte."

I opened the door to our balcony. There was only room for one person to stand, tightly wedged, between the wall and the rail

I looked up at the moon and stars, then gazed straight ahead, expecting to see the beautiful woods that had been described to us. I saw a shrub. One shrub. And beyond the shrub was another building. I opened the door and told Gloria to add "our balcony overlooking the woods" to the list of missing amenities.

The person who had made our reservation offered to refund our money. We were already there, however, and no other rooms were available anywhere on the strip. We were sure she probably knew that, so we accepted our towels and washcloths and called a truce, at least for the night.

We washed off our makeup, and put on honey oatmeal mudpacks. And after changing into our pajamas, we decided to make the best of it and see if there was a good movie on television. Gloria grabbed the remote and began pressing the channel button.

But the only channel we could get was the Home Shopping Network. As our faces hardened, we decided to watch it for a while. It was our first HSN experience. They were selling jewelry containing a stone we had never heard of. The hostess began to give insights into the African caves from which the stones were mined. We were spellbound and totally entertained until we both slipped into a deep slumber.

When we woke up the next morning, HSN was still on and we still had most of our oatmeal masks intact. As we began to stir, we decided that the events of the previous night had begun to take on elements of the *Twilight Zone*. We even checked behind possible locations for a hidden camera, just to make sure we weren't the victims of a *Candid Camera* prank.

Hungry and anxious to get showered, we dressed and went to eat a nice, hearty breakfast. But just as we were ready to leave the room, it hit both of us at the same time—we hadn't seen our ocean view yet! So we flung open the drapes. We started from as far left as we could see and slowly panned toward the right as far as our necks would crane. All we saw were hotel buildings.

"Wait," I said to Gloria. "Look!" I tilted my head to the side and pointed to a small patch of blue in between two of the buildings. "I think that's the ocean," I exclaimed, in the tone of a true explorer.

We felt like we'd been had. The descriptions we had been given of our accommodations were absolutely nothing like the reality of our surroundings. What a ripoff!

Things changed, however, as we ventured around Laguna and

soon we forgot our gripes as our day began to fill with joy. We savored a lobster omelet with a small stack of granola pancakes and a latte that was amazing. The art exhibits were wonderful. The shops were magnificent. At one point in the day, I rounded a corner, and there stood Gloria holding a sunflower she had purchased to brighten up our room, or as we called it, "the palace."

Gloria wanted to read by the pool, so I headed for the ocean. I contoured a body cave in the sand and got very comfortable drinking my bottled water and enjoying the sights. People were playing. Parents strolled with their children. Pet lovers walked their dogs. Old men played checkers. Teenagers played Frisbee. Children built sandcastles. Lovers walked hand in hand and occasionally stopped to kiss. I watched seagulls, boats, blue skies, and the ocean. I couldn't recall the last time I had been this relaxed. My hair was bleaching out and my skin was tanning. It was a beautiful day.

Gloria wandered down to join me around seven. The sunset was awesome. We watched it as though we had purchased expensive tickets for a concert with limited seating. The hues of purple, orange, peach, and yellow covered the horizon. A cool breeze rustled our clothes as we watched a lone sailboat move slowly through our panoramic view. A family of dolphins playfully made their way across the stage as seagulls dived for dinner. The percussive sounds of the ocean crashing onto the sand were intoxicatingly peaceful. We watched until the skies faded to black.

Our second night had been very different from the first one. We'd forgotten about the mace. The number of towels and the condition of our mattresses didn't seem to matter anymore. Although our television had been repaired, we didn't turn it on, and the balcony remained unvisited. With little conversation, we turned out the lights and crawled into our respective beds.

We realized we no longer had concern for anything that had gone wrong. Throughout the day, God had removed our frustration and replaced it by flooding our senses with His many gifts.

We were at perfect peace as the sounds of the ocean crashing against the sand rhythmically lulled us to sleep.

Sometimes the mundane frustrations of our lives can obscure our view of the bigger picture. At these times, it's good to step back and allow the beauty of God's masterful creation to soothe us. The key is learning that with the Creator as our guide, we can have an "ocean view" experience at any time and at any place. Not just in Laguna.

❀ ❀ ❀

Then God said, "Let the waters under the heavens be gathered together into one place, and let the dry land appear"; and so it was. And God called the dry land Earth, and the gathering together of the waters He called Seas. And God saw that it was good.

GENESIS 1:9–10

A Special Touch

Alveda Celeste King is the niece of Dr. Martin Luther King, Jr. and daughter of slain civil rights activist A. D. King. She has served four years in the Georgia State House of Representatives. Alveda founded King for America, Inc., a nonprofit organization that assists people in enriching their lives spiritually, personally, mentally, and economically. She says, "Faith in God and the commitment to fulfill His will for our lives—not government bureaucracy—is the key to positive action!"

I met Alveda through my long-time friend, vocalist Colette Robinson. Alveda and I formed an instant sisterhood and have lunched and met on several occasions since then. When she enters a room, you can immediately feel the presence of God walking in with her.

❀ ❀ ❀

DURING THE YEARS OF THE CIVIL RIGHTS MOVEMENT led by her uncle, Dr. Martin Luther King Jr., Alveda's family home in Birmingham, Alabama, was bombed, along with her father's church offices.

"I accepted Jesus as my Savior at a very young age and was baptized at the age of five," Alveda reflects. "However, from early childhood until adulthood and although I knew a lot of facts about God the Creator, God the Judge, and was aware of His presence, I never took the time to really get to know Him in a personal way.

210

"I went off to college and earned an undergraduate degree with a focus in the areas of journalism and sociology. I went on to earn a master of arts in business management from Central Michigan University.

"In 1983, I took a job teaching at Atlanta Metropolitan College. One of the other instructors at the school carried around a huge red Bible, and many of the other teachers warned me not to talk to her because she was a religious fanatic."

One day, when Alveda was alone in a classroom with the woman, Alveda said to her, "You know most of the teachers here call you a fanatic and I'd like to know why."

As the two began to talk, the woman said to Alveda, "Who's Jesus?"

Alveda began to answer her with facts: "He was born of the Virgin Mary. He's the Son of God. He died on the cross for our sins. He rose from the dead on the third day."

The woman asked again, "Who's Jesus?"

Alveda answered by continuing to give her facts about Jesus: "He was a teacher. He healed the sick. He raised the dead."

A third time the woman asked, "Who's Jesus?"

Frustrated and irritated, Alveda said, "I guess He's God!" Alveda then placed her hands on both hips and said, "Well, I guess I know He's God!"

As those words came out of her mouth, the reality of that truth sank deep into Alveda's spirit. From that moment on, Alveda began to ask the woman questions and the woman answered her, not with her own words, but with passages from her Bible.

That conversation created a hunger in Alveda and she began studying the Bible as though it was food for her soul. As a result, her relationship with the Lord deepened. Alveda began to see the character of God as loving, merciful, and caring.

Then big things began to happen in Alveda's life.

She became a published author with a best seller titled *I Don't Want Your Man, I Want My Own*. This inspirational collection of Christian testimonies is now being used at conferences and workshops around the world.

Alveda relays, "I was honored as a Senior Fellow at the Alexis de Tocqueville Institute and began serving on the boards of numerous community organizations. I ran for and was elected to the Georgia State House of Representatives, where I served for four years. I attribute every success I've ever had to the goodness and favor of the Lord!

"Now closing in on the half-century mark, I walk with God and know the Word of God. I believe in God the Father, God the Son, and God the Holy Spirit. I believe that He is the Alpha and Omega, the first and the last, who is and is to come.

But even with all of her confidence in God, one particular morning Alveda needed special attention from Him. And she needed it right then.

Sometimes Alveda's daughter would climb up in Alveda's lap and whisper, "I don't feel loved. I need a hug and some special attention." Alveda felt that on this particular morning. Although she had experienced the miracles and blessings of God, she needed a special touch from Him. Her past track record with God made her confident that before the day was out, He would be near to her.

Alveda's day began by attending a retirement party at her office. During the party, a guest soloist sang "His Eye Is on the Sparrow." Alveda was moved to tears as she left the event to attend the funeral of a little boy who had been killed in a car accident. At the funeral service, one of the songs that was sung was "His Eye Is on the Sparrow."

Later that evening, Alveda and her mother attended a combination anniversary and engagement party. A mother was celebrating her fortieth wedding anniversary and her daughter, an upcoming marriage. They had scheduled a romantic song to be performed during the party. But when the soloist stood to perform the song, she said, "I didn't have time to learn the song. May I just say something?"

Everyone began saying, "Just sing something you know." And so, with no musical accompaniment, the words began to spill from her lips, "Why do I feel discouraged? Why do the shadows come?"

As she got to the chorus, "I sing because I'm happy, I sing because I'm free. For His eye is on the sparrow and I know He watches me," Alveda realized that throughout the day, the Lord had been giving her that special touch she had needed from Him.

"As I've developed into a mature Christian my main desire is basking in the presence of God every second of every day.

"Anytime that we need a special touch from God, He will always comply. In such a tender way, He reminded me that if His eye is on the sparrow, He certainly watches over me. He eagerly desires to commune with each of us in every moment of every day.

✿ ✿ ✿

One thing I have desired of the LORD, that I will seek: that I may dwell in the house of the LORD all the days of my life, to behold the beauty of the LORD and to inquire in His temple. For in the time of trouble He shall hide me in His pavilion; in the secret place of His tabernacle He shall hide me: shall set me high upon a rock: Hear O LORD; when I cry with my voice! Have mercy also upon me, and answer me. When You said, "Seek my face," my heart said to You, Your face "LORD I will seek." Do not hide Your face from me; do not turn your face away in anger; You have been my help Do not leave me nor forsake me, O God of my salvation.

PSALM 27:4–5, 7–9

213

ALWAYS THERE

Born in Chillicothe, Ohio, Nancy Wilson knew at a young age that her voice would be the legacy she would share with the world.

By the mid-sixties, Nancy Wilson had risen to become one of Capitol Records' bestselling artists, second only to the Beatles. In 1964, she won a Grammy for her album *How Glad I Am* and went on to win an Emmy for her 1967-68 NBC Television Network series *The Nancy Wilson Show*.

Ms. Wilson's humanitarian efforts include the Cancer Society, the National Heart Association, the United Negro College Fund, the NAACP, Urban League, and the Martin Luther King Center for Social Change. She has received an Image Award, an Essence Award, and a Paul Robeson Humanitarian Award.

Ms. Wilson has a star on the Hollywood Walk of Fame, a street named for her, and has recently completed her sixtieth album.

For as long as I can remember, her music was always a part of my life.

Because my work is in the entertainment field, I've had opportunity to meet many celebrities through the years. But when I met Ms. Wilson, I was starstruck.

I'm not certain who referred me to her, but by mistake I was given her personal phone number rather than the number of her publicist. When I called the number to explain the project and get a fax number so that I could send a written overview, the voice message on the other end was unmistakably Nancy Wilson's.

It was such an honor for me to speak with Nancy Wilson. She was kind and approachable and the experience was one of those presents from God that I will remember always.

❁ ❁ ❁

FROM HER CHILDHOOD YEARS, Nancy Wilson learned to let every stumbling block become a stepping stone. For instance, when attending church with her stepmother as a little girl, she was told that because she sang secular music, she was not welcome to sing in the church choir. Nancy knew she had given her heart to the Lord and that she belonged to Him. Even the unfair treatment by the church that prohibited her from singing in the choir never caused her to doubt God's love and care for her.

Nancy also never doubted that God had gifted her with the ability to sing. So she simply went down the street to another church whose policy it was to let all God's children make a joyful noise.

Nancy explains, "I believe in God and in the gift that He gave me. God has been a pervasive, all-encompassing part of my life. I have always sensed His presence and know that no matter what, God is always there for me."

Her pilgrimage on this planet has God's fingerprints and favor all over it! At fifteen, Nancy's high school sponsored a talent contest. They asked her not to participate in it because if she did, they knew she would take the prize, hands down. However, she ended up representing her school in a local talent contest and won. The prize was getting her own television show where she sang twice a week for fifteen minutes each time.

"Although it would seem that having one's own television show would be somewhat intimidating and might pose an enormous amount of responsibility for a fifteen-year-old, I never gave it much thought. It was what I wanted. It was Phase One of a life-long dream that had come true and I never looked back."

Nancy began singing everywhere she could and soon landed a recording contract. She found herself in the company of such musical greats as Frank Sinatra, Cannonball Adderly, and Peggy Lee.

It's easy to see why she states with confidence that throughout her life, she has never doubted that God is always there.

" No matter what, God *is* always there, faithfully providing for our every need!"

Just like Nancy Wilson says in her soft, sultry way and with the confidence of one who has lived the experienced . . . "No matter what we need, God is always there!"

❀ ❀ ❀

Trust in the LORD, and do good; dwell in the land, and feed on His faithfulness. Delight yourself in the LORD; and He shall give you the desires of your heart. Commit your way to the LORD, Trust in Him, and He shall bring it to pass.

PSALM 37:3–5

216

Second Wind

Marty Magehee is a member of the popular contemporary Christian group 4Him. The group has had twenty #1 radio hits, a gold album, a Grammy nomination, six Dove Awards, and a trip to Russia with their sponsor, the American Bible Society. 4Him has performed over one thousand concert dates all over the world.

I first met Marty when 4Him cut one of my songs. Through the years, Marty and I have run into each other at various events. He is one of the funniest people I know and every time I'm with him I make him do his profile-imitation of the "Grinch That Stole Christmas." He's hysterical!

I interviewed Marty by phone while he was at home in Nashville with his wife and two boys.

I T WAS SEPTEMBER 19,1994, when 4Him member Marty and his wife Sherry were in St. Lucia, West Indies, enjoying a second honeymoon.

On their second evening there, Marty awakened in the middle of the night with severe chills. His teeth were chattering and his legs felt like blocks of ice. It was an eerie occurrence in such a warm tropical setting.

Marty also felt some strange circulation sensations in his legs. In an attempt to restore some of his body heat and stop him from shaking, Sherry wrapped her body around him. Finally Marty fell asleep.

The next morning, Marty's left ankle had swollen to the size of a grapefruit. The pain was excruciating. Marty explains, "I had gone diving the day before. The undertow had pulled me into a den of black crow quilled sea urchins. They are extremely poisonous and the venom from a small sting can actually rot off entire limbs. I hadn't considered the possibility that I had been stung, thinking that perhaps I had injured my ankle when I crashed into the coral cave."

Throughout the day, Marty's ankle got worse. By the following day, the swelling had moved up to his knee, prohibiting him from straightening his leg.

Four days later, as they were leaving to return to the States, Marty couldn't walk without assistance. He was using an umbrella as a makeshift cane. He decided not to see a doctor in the islands, but to wait until they returned home to have an examination.

"Over the next few weeks, I saw ten other doctors. I was diagnosed with everything from gout to Lyme disease to a male form of lupus. By this time, the swelling had migrated to my right ankle, right knee, right collarbone, and right wrist."

Unbelievably, the eleventh doctor Marty went to had had the same condition and was able to give him a correct diagnosis. Marty had inherited a genetic disorder, a B-27 antigen, from his mother's side of the family. When coupled with a bacterial infection, which could have very well been a prick from the quill of one of the sea urchins, the antigen exploded and spread throughout his body, affecting random joints. Marty was told that it is a degenerative disorder and that there's no cure. He was also told he would have this condition for the rest of his life.

"I spent the next month and a half in a wheelchair. I lost about thirty-five pounds of muscle weight and my legs atrophied. I began trying to exercise to build back some of my muscle, but it was next to impossible."

"I continued to travel with 4Him, performing at all of their concert dates, sometimes with a cane, other times in a wheelchair. The most difficult task of all was going down stairs because it took the most muscle control. I was in constant, excruciating pain."

Four months after Marty was diagnosed, 4Him was performing a concert at an Assembly of God Church in Pittsburgh. After the concert, a woman Marty had never met approached him. Many different people had come up to Marty and had told him that God had sent them with a message for him, so he was a little skeptical of whatever the woman was about to say.

But Marty immediately knew the woman was truly sent from the Lord when her first words were, "Marty, you don't know me and I don't know you, but God told me you are a runner."

She had Marty's undivided attention because he loved to run and had been a runner all of his life.

She continued, "By this, I don't mean in the physical. The Lord showed me that you are a runner in the spirit realm. He told me to tell you not to be discouraged, because your second wind is coming. When it comes, it will be at a time when you are running so fast toward God that before you know it, you'll turn around and realize you're not in pain anymore."

Marty continues, "Three months after hearing the word from God through this woman, 4Him was performing at a church in Indiana. I began walking to the stage from the dressing room. I had to walk down two flights of stairs with a landing in between them before I would reach the main floor and the stage entrance."

"When I reached the landing, something occurred to me. I couldn't remember if I had felt any pain as I descended the first flight of stairs. I looked at the next flight and consciously went down them. I felt no pain whatsoever."

When Marty reached the bottom of the stairs, his head was reeling. He had been dealing with so much pain for the last seven months, he was stunned at the possibility that it could be gone. But it was.

Marty got on stage with the rest of the group. As Mark introduced the first song, Marty pulled Kirk aside and told him to squeeze his foot. As he did, Marty laughed and said, "I don't feel any pain."

As Andy introduced the next song, Marty pulled Mark behind a stack of speakers and had him do the same thing. Needless to say, the guys weren't exactly sure what to think, but they were all elated!

Following the concert, one of their board members, Tim Burke, put his arm around Marty and commented on how great he seemed to be doing. Marty looked at Tim and said for the first time, "God healed me tonight."

"As soon as those words came out of my mouth, I began to cry uncontrollably. On my way back to the dressing room, I passed an unfinished room that harbored the church air conditioners. Wanting to have a moment alone, I entered the room and just praised God. There was no one to hug, so I hugged the unplastered walls. I jumped up and down and danced with my hands lifted high in the air, thanking God for healing me."

He opened the door and made his way down the hall to the dressing room. As he entered the room, the rest of the guys were startled by his appearance. Marty had his coat off, his eyes were red, his hair was all messed up, and he had sheetrock dust on his forehead. Marty looked at them and said for the second time, "Guys, God healed me tonight!"

When they all returned to their bus that night, they spent about half an hour just thanking God for such a major blessing. Then Andy challenged Marty to a footrace.

They jumped off the bus and ran around in the parking lot. Because Marty's legs felt like wet noodles and were still atrophied, Andy won the race. But for Marty, it was much more than that. As he ran, he felt the wind in his face. It was at that point when Marty's thoughts turned to the words of the woman sent by God: "One day, you'll suddenly realize that you're no longer in pain. God has promised to give you a second wind."

Marty Magehee was rejoicing and grateful that such a day

had come, that he was walking without pain and basking in the amazing gift of his second wind.

❀ ❀ ❀

You shall tread upon the lion and the cobra, the young lion and the serpent you shall trample underfoot. Because he has set his love upon Me, therefore I will deliver him; I will set you on high, because he has known My name. He will call upon Me and I will answer him. I will be with him in times of trouble; I will deliver him and honor him.

PSALM 91:13–15

LIVING PROOF

Ben Vereen is internationally known as a premiere entertainer in television, film, and stage. He's won numerous awards
for his roles in *Pippin*, *Jelly's Last Jam*, *Sweet Charity*, *Hair*,
and *Jesus Christ Superstar*. Recently, he's been a guest star on
Touched by an Angel, *Second Noah*, *The Nanny*, *New York
Undercover*, *Fresh Prince of Bel Air*, and *Star Trek: The Next
Generation*. He will always be remembered for his role as
Chicken George in the seven-time Emmy Award-winning
miniseries, *Roots*.

Ben has appeared in the feature films *All That Jazz* and *Funny
Girl*. He was the first entertainer to win three AGVA awards in
the same year: Entertainer of the Year, Rising Star, and Song and
Dance Star. He has chaired the American Heart Association, the
Sudden Infant Death Syndrome Association, and Celebrities for
a Drug-free America. Of his many humanitarian involvements,
the one closest to his heart is the Kids to Kids Prevention Program, which is an educational arts abuse-prevention program.

I interviewed Mr. Vereen as he watched the showroom fill up
for his 10 P.M. performance in Las Vegas. His high energy and
enthusiasm for life came through the phone lines and converted
my midnight eastern time to daybreak! I was thrilled to get to
interview such a legacy.

❀ ❀ ❀

I N HIS SEARCH FOR TRUTH, Ben Vereen has tried all the religions—Baptist, Pentecostal, Catholic, Buddhism, and Muslim. In fact, there are very few philosophies he hasn't entertained in an effort to know the One and True Living God.

The conclusion to this lifelong investigation revealed many things to Ben. One of those nuggets is that God is so awesome and magnificent that it is difficult to tag Him with a name defined by human terms. Mere words cannot adequately and effectively encompass God's majesty and greatness, or the full essence of His character

Prior to 1992, Ben had studied with many great teachers like Johnnie Coleman, Michael Beckwith, and Benny Hinn, each of whom had taught him that we are all vessels created by our Maker. When we open ourselves up to have the power that God breathed into us, what He can accomplish through us can be quite something.

Ben took the knowledge he'd gleaned from his mentors and began traveling throughout the country conducting speaking engagements where he told his audiences of the wonderful power of the Most High God. Ben taught about many issues of life. He spoke of how the Bible, as well as other wonderful books, had been used as keys to his awareness of God. He shared that we have unlimited potential when we're empowered by the Spirit of God and how the still small voice in all of us was the inner connection to God. But to that point, all of his exhortation was hypothetical and in theory only. He was really just a spectator tying to tell others how it is to actually play in the game.

But all of that would change.

One evening, Ben was driving along the highway and, without remembering how it happened, his car hit a tree. The impact of the accident caused him to hit his head on the roof of his car, damaging an artery to his brain.

Unable to detect his internal injuries and without the knowledge that he had actually suffered a stroke, Ben went with the officers to the precinct to complete an accident report and answer some routine questions. As the proceedings got under way, Ben remembers joking with some of the officers because he was set to be a headliner at an upcoming benefit they were involved in together.

After leaving the police station, he went to his manager's house for a while. About 3 A.M. Ben decided to walk home.

On his way home, a truck hit him.

There were no phones in the area of road where Ben was hit. Thankfully, the man who hit him had a phone in his truck and dialed 911. Almost immediately, helicopters and emergency vehicles arrived on the scene.

Ben remembers, "When I woke up in the hospital, I didn't remember the first accident when I hit the tree, or the second one when I was hit by the truck. All I remember is waking from a beautiful dream where I felt I was carried by someone."

The first person he saw when he opened he eyes was his daughter. Ben thought to himself, What is she doing here? She's supposed to be in college in Boston.

"Next, I noticed my leg had been broken and was in some sort of an apparatus. I'd had a stroke on my right side, my spleen had been removed, and I had a tracheotomy that prohibited me from speaking.

"For someone who had spent his life making a living as a singer and a dancer, my condition looked beyond bleak. As far as I could assess, I thought life as I had known it was over."

Unknown to him, however, at that same time there were people all over the world on their knees before God, petitioning the throne of God with their prayers.

In an almost inaudible whisper, one of the first things Ben asked was what his recovery chances were. The answer was not what he had hoped to hear. He was told that he would probably never sing again and that if he was able to walk at all, it would take several years of extensive therapy and that even then, he would probably always walk with a cane.

"Almost instantly, I began to call up in my spirit all the truths

I had spoken to others; "Whenever I am afraid, I will trust in You." (Psalm 56:3); "I will bless the Lord at all times. His praise will continually be in my mouth." (Psalm 34:1); "Now David was greatly distressed . . . but David strengthened himself in the Lord his God." (1 Samuel 30:6)

"I immediately resolved that if God had a plan for me that involved a wheelchair and no voice, I was fine with that. But I also knew if God's plan was to heal me, my healing had already been determined before my car hit the tree. I knew that either way, one thing was for certain: In and of myself I could do nothing."

Ben began to pray, "God I can't do anything about this, but You can. You made all of my parts in the first place, so You can make them new again. I've been telling everybody else of Your greatness and Your capabilities for perfect healing power, so now here I am standing in the need of prayer. Please do this great thing in my life. Help me, heal me!"

"I knew God could heal me, but I also realized that for God to heal me, *I* had to show up. On numerous occasions, I had seen people ask God for things like healing, jobs, mending broken relationships, but in those situations, those asking for God's help did nothing themselves." I had emphatically instructed them, "If you want a job, you're going to probably have to get up and leave your house. If you want a severed relationship healed, it will take work and effort. If you want God to heal you, you have to exercise your faith.

"So I committed to work with every angel God sent my way—doctors, nurses, therapists, and technicians alike. I came to the understanding that God had actually chosen each of these professionals to be at this specific place and at this specific time. God's sole plan in bringing this ensemble together there was to accomplish His purpose through their expertise in bringing about a miracle in my life!"

And so it would be.

Only ten months after he was admitted to the hospital with

multiple injuries and little hope for a full recovery, Ben Vereen walked onto a Broadway stage, where he performed one of the leading roles in *Jelly's Last Jam,* a musical packed with dancing and singing.

When our faith collides with God's power, miracles occur and Ben Vereen is living proof it is so.

❀ ❀ ❀

I waited patiently and expectantly for the LORD; and He inclined to me and heard my cry. He drew me up out of a horrible pit, out of the miry clay, and set my feet upon a rock, steadying my steps and establishing my goings. And He has put a new song in my mouth, a song of praise to our God; Many shall see and fear (revere and worship) and will put their trust and confident reliance in the LORD.

PSALM 40:1–3, THE AMPLIFIED BIBLE

Nurse's Bait

At barely five feet tall and weighing eighty-seven pounds soaking wet, octogenarian Madge Yoakley has the energy and enthusiasm of someone half her age.

The unofficial chaplain at Good Samaritan Hospital in West Palm Beach, Florida, Madge spends a portion of every day visiting patients, offering hope through prayer, and winning over everyone who comes under the influence of her million-dollar smile.

We first met the day she came bolting into my father's hospital room, greeting us with a grand "Good morning!" and carrying a decorative bowl of peppermints that she referred to as "nurse's bait."

My dad's room was filled with well-wishers and Madge said she wouldn't stay, but simply lifted her hand and began to pray in the name of Jesus over everyone present. Then she left the nurse's bait for all to enjoy.

My father spent many weeks at Good Samaritan during his yearlong fight with cancer. Madge made our days brighter and seeing her was always a highlight for my family and me.

MANY PATIENTS AT THE HOSPITAL have no visitors other than Madge. On Sundays, her visit was oftentimes "church" for many of them. She consistently and faithfully brings the love of Christ to the patients at Good Sam.

Madge Yoakley is the highest example of what it means to be a true servant of God.

In addition to her duties as a chaplain, Madge has taught a Bible study at the Royal Poinsettia Chapel in Palm Beach every Wednesday for the past twenty-four years. Each week, just as the Bible study convenes, Madge introduces all of the visitors in the group.

One particular day, a young African-American couple stood to introduce themselves. The young man said, "Mrs. Yoakley, I'm sure you don't remember me, but I certainly remember you!

"Fifteen years ago when I was five years old, my family was in a terrible car accident. We were in the hospital for many weeks. I remember you coming by every day to see us, praying for us and bringing us bowls full of peppermint candies. As I recall, you referred to them as nurse's bait. The love and concern you extended to my family ministered to us in ways you'll never know. You were the first person to show me the true and consistent love of God."

He continued, "I wanted you to know that I have totally given my life to the Lord and right now I'm at Palm Beach Atlantic College studying to be a minister. When we knew we were coming back to this area, one of my first goals was to look you up. I wanted to let you know what an impact you had on my life and that my decision to go into the ministry came at a very early age due to your fine example. I wanted to thank you for serving the Lord."

A little flushed, Madge's eyes began to fill with tears. She modestly thanked the young man for his kind words and then quickly moved ahead to other matters, so as not to draw anymore attention to herself.

Madge Yoakley has touched the lives of many and has loved people as Christ has loved her for all of her life. All of the fruit that has come from her obedience to her Lord is impossible to accurately calculate. But because of the way she allows God to use her, a five-year-old boy felt the love of God and that experience forever changed his life.

❀ ❀ ❀

Go therefore and make disciples of all the nations, baptizing them in the name of the Father and of the Son and of the Holy Spirit, teaching them to observe all things that I have commanded you; and lo, I am with you always, even to the end of the age.

MATTHEW 28:19–20

GREAT IS THY FAITHFULNESS

With two records to her credit, Deborah Cox is well on her way to becoming a major success in the music industry. Her second album, *One Wish*, is breaking records left and right. The first single, *You're Not Supposed to Be Here*, stayed at #1 on the Billboard charts for fourteen weeks. At the time of our interview, her second single, *It's Over Now*, was soaring to the top of the charts as well. Deborah attends Spreading the Word Ministries in Southern California.

I met Deborah through her manager, Miguel Melendez, who arranged the interview.

Jet-lagged, Deborah graciously granted a phone interview from Los Angeles the day after she returned home from a concert tour in Germany. I found her to be vibrant, focused, and a true visionary. She seems to be a woman of character who knows what she wants and seeks strategies ordained of God to get there. Deborah is very mindful of the platform entrusted to her and desires to glorify God by representing Him well in every aspect of her life. Yea, Deborah! I pray she sells a gazillion records!

❀ ❀ ❀

FROM THE TIME SHE WAS NINE YEARS OLD, Toronto, Canada, native and R&B singing sensation Deborah Cox knew that her life's work would be spent as a singer and songwriter. As is the case with many young girls having the same dream, she spent hours practicing in front of a mirror in an effort to polish the talent she knew would one day take her to the top.

"God was always someone I thought of and prayed to, but when I reached my high school years, I began doing a little more investigation into knowing God at a more personal level. Many of my friends were church goers or involved in Bible studies, but it seemed to me that many of my friends had somehow missed the whole point in developing a relationship with the Lord.

"For many of my friends, it seemed that the main transition to occur in their lives in attempting to know God was that they had to give up everything they had been doing prior to their decision to follow Him. This, of course, included singing any type of music that wasn't a hymn. I couldn't buy into that philosophy. In my assessment, God had created music and had certainly not limited it to one particular kind. That train of thought was like looking at all of the variety of flowers God created and being allowed to have daisies only.

"I couldn't believe such limited thinking could possibly be God's plan, but as a youngster, I wasn't exactly sure what God's plan was or what my relationship with Him would be. But I definitely knew one thing for certain . . . I wanted to pursue a career in music.

"After graduation from high school, I never turned away from God. I knew He was always there. Every night I would pray a prayer my father gave to me: 'I thank Thee, oh Lord, for the day I have passed. Bless the night, oh Lord, and protect me. Into Thine hands I commend my spirit and body. Bless my parents, relatives, brothers, sisters, and friends. Guide us into Thy path and make us one with Thee. Amen'

"I didn't know how or when my dreams would come true, but I leaned on God and put my faith in His abilities and not my own. I trusted that if a music career was in His plan for my life, it would indeed come to pass.

"There wasn't a huge R&B community in Canada, but my writing partner, Lascellas, and I didn't let that discourage us. We knew from reading the Bible, that 'faith without works is dead.'

(James 2:17) and that 'faith is the substance of things hoped for, and the evidence of things not seen.' (Hebrews 11:1), so we set a goal to write one song a week. Each week, we mailed as much material as possible to a list of record companies we had compiled. We began making trips to Los Angeles and New York to pitch our songs."

Finally their efforts paid off when a producer they met got them a meeting with the president of Arista Records, Clive Davis. A record deal was struck and Deborah was on her way.

Her first self-titled record saw admirable success. But then came the time to begin selecting material for her second record. Deborah had a new management team and she and Lascelles joined a new church, Spreading the Word Ministries. There they found incredible teaching and imparting of the Word which would help them grow as Christians, and a congregation who offered a constant prayer covering to them.

"This is when I really felt my life begin to turn around. My trust and faith in the Lord deepened as I learned to completely trust in God and not lean on any of my own senses. My pastor taught me about tithing and other principles that work so profoundly in the spirit world. Any stress, pressure, or anxiousness I felt in pulling together my new record soon dissipated.

"I learned not just to act like a Christian, but to live like a Christian, that by putting God first, everything else would fall into place.

"We began selecting songs for my new record, titled *One Wish*. There was one song in particular that I really believed in and really wanted to record. It was called 'Nobody's Supposed to Be Here.'

"I knew I needed to record this song, but many obstacles seemed to arise in seeing that desire come to fruition. Originally, I was to have recorded the song with God's Property and that didn't work out. Then we had to go back and forth to secure the song to record because there were several other artists who liked it, too."

Finally, Clive Davis called to say that they had secured the

232

song. After the record was completed, Arista held a listening party for industry and radio representatives to get their take on which songs would be the strongest to release as singles.

Deborah was rooting for "Nobody's Supposed to Be Here" to be released as a single. But even Clive Davis, who is internationally known for his ability to pick great songs, didn't seem to be as sold on that particular song as he was on some of the other material. In fact, he considered not even playing it for the meeting. But he changed his mind and when he played it, everyone in the room went crazy over the song Deborah had fought so hard to have on her record.

"My manager brought my record before his church congregation, and they prayed over its release and success. My church family and I also prayed and asked God to let it go to #1."

"Nobody's Supposed to Be Here" became Deborah's first single and set a record by staying at #1 on the R&B radio charts for fourteen weeks! It was beyond all that she had dreamed.

As Deborah looks back on where she's come from and looks forward to where God's taking her, she is reminded of the words to an old standard hymn that summarizes the gratitude in her heart:

Great is Thy faithfulness, oh God my Father
Morning by morning new mercies I see.
All I have needed Thy hand hath provided.
Great is Thy faithfulness, Lord unto me.

Through the LORD's mercies we are not consumed, because His compassions fail not. They are new every morning; Great is Your faithfulness.

LAMENTATIONS 3:22–23

233

ONLY TEMPORARY

Stormie Omartian has authored eight books *including Stormie, The Power of a Praying Wife*, and *Just Enough Light for the Step I'm On*. She is a highly sought-after speaker for conferences, seminars and retreats, and has also been featured in five exercise videos, several of which have gone Gold.

Recently she and her husband Michael completed a Christmas musical *called The Child of the Promise*, starring Michael Crawford, Donna Summer, Crystal Lewis, Steven Curtis Chapman, Vince Gill, Howard Hewitt, Bob Carlisle, Gary Chapman, David Pack, Richard Marx, and a host of others. It will be released as a recording and as a television special, and will also be performed throughout the country as a live stage production.

I met Stormie through our mutual friend Sarah Dowdy and interviewed her by phone from her home in Nashville.

❀ ❀ ❀

WHETHER IT BE FINANCIAL PROBLEMS, the death of a loved one, failing health, or a misplaced job opportunity, throughout our lives we will all suffer losses. When such an experience occurs, the feeling of emptiness can be overwhelming. Such was the case for Stormie Omartian when she suffered the loss of her lifelong best friend, Diane.

Stormie and Diane met while in high school. They were both artistic and enjoyed participating in several school plays together. They also told each other their deepest and darkest secrets, including the fact that Stormie's mom suffered from mental illness and that Diane's mom was an alcoholic. Both girls felt the shame and fear that come from living in constant dysfunction. Their emptiness and isolation created a common bond that drew them to each other. Each was able to openly and honestly discuss their fears and feelings of hopelessness, knowing that the other understood only too well. Finding solace in friendship was like finding an oasis in the desert. Stormie could say two words and Diane could complete the sentence. They were soul mates.

Although they had attended different colleges, after graduation they landed back in the same city and became roommates in their first apartment. Stormie and Diane did what so many other young people have done . . . they tried to fill the void in their lives with "things." They experimented with drugs and alcohol, partied at every opportunity and embraced new ideas and philosophies. Both got into the New Age movement and dabbled in the occult but were left feeling empty, with no meaning or purpose.

Then something happened.

"I started visiting The Church on the Way pastored by Jack Hayford," Stormie said, "and soon came to an understanding of what had been missing in my life—a personal relationship with Jesus Christ.

"I was elated to have received the free gift of forgiveness for my sins and salvation through placing my faith and trust in Christ. Finally I made the connection that in my own ability and strength I could not right my wrongs, but that Jesus had done that for me."

For a while, Stormie's newfound truth put an awkwardness in her relationship with Diane. Stormie was experiencing something that Diane didn't understand. But Stormie kept sharing what she was learning with her beloved friend until eventually, Diane converted to Christianity also.

Later in life, they both married and started families at about the same time. Diane's son, John, was born two years after Stormie's son, Christopher, and two years before her daughter, Amanda.

The two women's lives were totally intermingled. From carpooling and celebrating birthdays and holidays, to going on vacations together, for as long as they could remember, they had always been inseparable. But a routine medical examination would change everything when Diane received the devastating news that she had terminal cancer.

"Initially, a flood of emotions rushed over us, encompassing everything from shock to denial to disbelief. How could this be? Diane was too young to be dying. Her son was only eight and he needed his mother. Her husband was the love of her life. And I couldn't be left without my best friend of twenty-eight years."

As hard as they prayed for a different outcome, Diane died. After the funeral Stormie felt such a thick sense of grief that it paralyzed her. When she woke up the day after Diane's funeral, she remembers having cried so fiercely that she had no more tears left. The lump in her throat felt like a permanent fixture. Her only thought was that no one would ever know her the way Diane had. Her loneliness was unbearable.

This sense of sadness, emptiness, and detachment lingered for months. Stormie felt as though she was missing a part of herself. She longed to reconnect with that irreplaceable friendship she had grown to know and love for all those years.

"I prayed constantly, asking God to remove my sadness. I was never without the lump in my throat and constantly felt as though I could easily burst into tears. Close to reaching a point of desperation, I cried out to God to show me how to survive this loss."

Stormie and her family moved into a new neighborhood about twenty minutes from where they had lived before. A few women from her church lived in the new neighborhood and came by to welcome her and her family.

During the conversation one of the ladies reached out to Stormie and said, "We know you lost your best friend, but we would really like to be friends with you and try to fill in the gap you're feeling. We know we can never replace Diane, but maybe between the three of us, each of us can bring a little piece of something to your life and together with all the different parts, maybe we could make up that whole area that's missing."

Stormie felt the visit had been an answer to prayer.

"A few days later another woman stopped by and told me she knew that as long as I lived, Diane would be my best friend, but that she wanted me to be her best friend. She told me there needn't be any reciprocity, that she didn't need to take Diane's place and be my best friend but that I would still be hers.

"Tears began to well up in my eyes as this angel disguised as a neighbor hugged me and wiped away my tears. Again, I knew that this had been an answer to prayer and that the Lord was encouraging me to open myself to others who were reaching out to me. With the words of my new friend, I felt something break off of me. It was a release of sorts, whispering into the ears of my heart the necessity to live my life."

Finally, the lump in her throat was gone.

Stormie is enjoying the gift God sent to her in the way of new friendships. She still misses Diane and often calls up the years of memories the two created during their lifelong friendship.

"But now when I reminisce, I look forward—not back, knowing with full assurance that we'll be reunited one day and that because of Christ, our separation is only temporary."

❀ ❀ ❀

But may the God of all grace, who called us to His eternal glory by Christ Jesus, after you have suffered a while will perfect, establish, strengthen and settle you.

1 PETER 5:10

237

GOD IS NOT JUST
A *LITTLE* SOVEREIGN!

WHEN BABBIE MASON AND I FIRST MET, her schedule was a whirlwind. Between her duties as a wife, a mom to two sons, teaching middle school fulltime, having twenty piano students, and performing at funerals, weddings, and concerts on the weekends, the phrase "living life to its fullest" was an understatement.

Babbie's goal was to eventually go into ministry fulltime and sign a recording contract with a Christian record label. Although several recording companies were courting her, she hadn't decided which one to go with. She was prayerfully waiting on clarity and God's perfect timing.

One Sunday morning, Babbie was the guest soloist at a local church. The governor of Georgia, Joe Frank Harris, was in the congregation. After hearing her sing and loving her voice, Governor Harris invited Babbie to sing at the Governor's Mansion for an upcoming prayer breakfast. When she arrived, she learned the keynote speaker was Cliff Barrows from the Billy Graham team.

Following her performance, Mr. Barrows extended an invitation for Babbie to sing at an upcoming Billy Graham Crusade. He told her he wanted her to sing an up-tempo song and asked her to send him several choices. Babbie mailed a tape with six up-tempo songs and, at the last minute, decided to put a ballad that I had written, "He'll Find A Way" as the seventh song on the tape. Much to our surprise and delight, "He'll Find A Way" was the one Mr. Barrows selected.

About three weeks after taping the Billy Graham Crusade in Tallahassee, Florida, Babbie received the devastating news that her father, Rev. George Wade, had suddenly died of a massive heart attack.

She left for Michigan to be with her family and to attend her dad's funeral. After the service, as everyone was gathered at Babbie's parents' home, someone turned on the television just in time to hear Cliff Barrows announce, "Please welcome to the Billy Graham Crusade, Babbie Mason."

As her family listened, grief-stricken over their loss and wondering how and when they would ever begin to get past it, God used Babbie singing "He'll Find A Way" to minister to her entire family, including herself:

> For I know that if He can paint a sunset and put the stars in place
> I know if He can raise up mountains and calm the storm-tossed waves
> And if He can conquer death forever to open heaven's gates
> I know for you, I know for you, He'll find a way

Ten years later, in August of 1996, my dad called to tell me that he had lung cancer and that within the next week he would have to have a portion of his left lung removed. After his surgery was completed, we were told that the operation was a success and that the doctors had removed all of the cancerous tissue.

A year later when his speech began to slur, he was diagnosed with brain cancer, the same type the lung cancer had been. Although the surgeons had elected not to do radiation or chemotherapy after his lung surgery, apparently some of the cancer cells had broken loose from his lungs and had now spread to his brain.

The brain tumor was removed and radiation was recommended. He went for treatments twice a day for thirty-seven days, walking in and out of his appointments without assistance.

Then without warning, he began to decline. By April of 1998, he was unable to walk or talk. In the months that followed his condition worsened.

Five days before my dad died on September 23, 1998, I was awakened one morning with some of the words to a new song. I called Babbie and as we completed writing it, I knew right then that the Lord had sent this song to us to be sung at my dad's funeral. It is called "I Can See You."

After Dad went to be with the Lord, the funeral arrangements were difficult to make because of a hurricane passing through Florida. We finally decided it would be on Saturday, September 26.

I wanted Babbie to fly down with me and sing at the service. Although Babbie's concert schedule is booked two years in advance and she is almost always singing or traveling on the weekends, it just so happened that she was off the Saturday of my dad's funeral.

When we arrived at the Atlanta airport to catch our plane to Palm Beach, Florida, my Bible mentors for the last fifteen years, Patsy and Al Rhodes, were sitting at our gate, headed to a convention in Palm Beach. Another long-time friend, Clyde Upchurch, was already in Palm Beach for the same convention. They were all able to be with me at my dad's service.

The service was scheduled for 3 P.M. but was announced in the paper at 3:30 P.M. Not wanting to begin without everyone there, Babbie sat down at the piano and sang a thirty-minute concert. Among many other selections, she sang "Amazing Grace," "What Can Separate?," "The Old Rugged Cross," "Blessed Assurance," and "He'll Find A Way." What a blessing she was!

Without ever having spoken to the pastor before the service, he used in his message several of the lines from the song we had just written, "I Can See You," and Babbie ended the service by singing it:

You've fought your fight, you've done your best
You've faced the fire and passed the test
But the time has come to let you go
You're finally free because you're finally home

I can see you walkin' on streets of gold
Singin' with the angels and the saints of old
I can see you at peace and finally whole
I can see you runnin' into the arms of Jesus

No more sickness, no more sorrow
No more sad days and hopeless tomorrows
No more tears, no more pain
For to live is Christ, and to die is gain

I can see you walkin' on streets of gold
Singin' with the angels and the saints of old
I can see you at peace and finally whole
I can see you runnin' into the arms of Jesus

The race that you've run is finally won
Well done, faithful servant, well done

Before God ever hung the first star, He had it all worked out. Babbie would sing at a church where the governor was worshipping. The governor would love her voice and invite her to sing at a prayer breakfast where Cliff Barrows was the keynote speaker. Cliff Barrows would invite Babbie to sing at a Billy Graham Crusade. Although he had asked Babbie to sing an up-tempo song, he chose the only ballad on her tape, "He'll Find A Way." The Billy Graham Crusade would air the night of Babbie's father's funeral and her singing "He'll Find A Way" would minister to her entire family.

Eleven years later, Babbie would not be booked on the Saturday of my father's funeral and would be able to accompany me

241

to his service and sing "He'll Find A Way" to my family. My Bible mentors who live in Atlanta would be on our same plane headed to a convention in Palm Beach and would be able to be with me at the funeral. The pastor who conducted my dad's funeral would use several of the lines from our new song, "I Can See You," in his message, because the same Holy Spirit that penned our song penned his sermon. Babbie would close the service with that same song.

God is a God of intricate detail. His ways are always flawless and His plans are always perfect. Although we can't see the whole picture, we can rest in these pearls of wisdom from the very lips of Babbie Mason: "God is not just a *little* Sovereign! "

O Lord, I will honor and praise Your name, for you are my God; You do such wonderful things. You planned them long ago and now You've accomplished them, just as you said!

ISAIAH 25:1, THE LIVING BIBLE

OTHER BOOKS BY STARBURST PUBLISHERS®

God Stories—
They're So Amazing, Only God Could Make Them Happen   *Donna I. Douglas*
Famous individuals share their personal, true-life experiences with God in this beautiful new book! Find out how God has touched the lives of top recording artists, professional athletes, and other newsmakers such as: Jessi Colter, Deana Carter, Ben Vereen, Stephanie Zimbalist, Cindy Morgan, Sheila E, Joe Jacoby, Cheryl Landon, Brett Butler, Clifton Taulbert, Babbie Mason, Michael Medved, Sandi Patty, Charlie Daniels, and more! Their stories are intimate, poignant, and sure to inspire and motivate you as you listen for God's message in your own life!
(cloth)   ISBN 1892016117   **$18.95**

More of Him, Less of Me   *Jan Christensen*
Subtitled: *A Daybook of My Personal Insights, Inspirations & Meditations on the Weigh Down™ Diet.* The insight shared in this year-long daybook of inspiration will encourage you on your weight-loss journey, bring you to a deeper relationship with God, and help you improve any facet of your life. Each page includes an essay, Scripture, and a tip-of-the-day that will encourage and uplift you as you trust God to help you achieve your proper weight. Perfect for companion guide for anyone on the Weigh Down™ diet!
(cloth)   ISBN 1892016001   **$17.95**

Seasons of a Woman's Heart—
A Daybook of Stories and Inspiration   *Compiled by Lynn D. Morrissey*
A woman's heart is complex. This daybook of stories, quotes, scriptures, and daily reflections will inspire and refresh. Christian women share their heart-felt thoughts on Seasons of Faith, Growth, Guidance, Nurturing, and Victory. Including Christian women's writers such as Kay Arthur, Emilie Barnes, Luci Swindoll, Jill Briscoe, Florence Littauer, and Gigi Graham Tchividjian.
(cloth)   ISBN 1892016036   **$18.95**

God's Abundance   *Edited by Kathy Collard Miller*
Over 100,000 sold! This day-by-day inspirational is a collection of thoughts by leading Christian writers such as Patsy Clairmont, Jill Briscoe, Liz Curtis Higgs, and Naomi Rhode. *God's Abundance* is based on God's Word for a simpler, yet more abundant life. Learn to make all aspects of your life—personal, business, financial, relationships, even housework a "spiritual abundance of simplicity."
(cloth)   ISBN 0914984977   **$19.95**

Stories of God's Abundance—
for a More Joyful Life   *Compiled by Kathy Collard Miller*
Like its successful predecessor, *God's Abundance* (100,000 sold), this book is filled with beautiful, inspirational, real-life stories. Those telling their stories of God share scriptures and insights that readers can apply to their daily lives. Renew your faith in life's small miracles and challenge yourself to allow God to lead the way as you find the source of abundant living for all your relationships.
(trade paper)   ISBN 1892016060   **$12.95**

God's Unexpected Blessings   *Edited by Kathy Collard Miller*
Over 50,000 sold! Learn to see the unexpected blessings in life. These individual essays describe experiences that seem negative on the surface but are something God has used for good in our lives or to benefit others. Witness God at work in our lives. Learn to trust God in action. Realize that we always have a choice to learn and benefit from these experiences by letting God prove His promise of turning all things for our good. (cloth)   ISBN 0914984071   **$18.95**

The Weekly Feeder—
A Revolutionary Shopping, Cooking and Meal Planning System   *Cori Kirkpatrick*
The Weekly Feeder is a revolutionary meal planning system that will make preparing home-cooked dinners more convenient than ever. At the beginning of each week, simply choose one of the eight pre-planned weekly menus, tear out the corresponding grocery list, do your shopping, and whip up a great meal in less than 45 minutes! The author's household management tips, equipment checklists, and nutrition information make this system a must have for any busy family. Also included with every recipe is a personal anecdote from the author emphasizing the importance of good food, a healthy family, and a well-balanced life.
(trade paper)   ISBN 1892016095   **$16.95**

Since Life Isn't a Game, These Are God's Rules—
Finding Joy & Happiness in God's Ten Commandments   *Kathy Collard Miller*
We often hear life being referred to as a *game*, but we know this is not really true. In life there is only one set of rules and those are God's. God gave us the Ten Commandments for our good—to protect and guide us. In this book, Kathy Collard Miller explains the meaning of each of the Ten Commandments and illustrates how they are relevant in today's life. Each chapter includes Scripture and quotes from some of our most beloved Christian authors including Billy Graham, Patsy Clairmont, Liz Curtis Higgs, and more! Sure to renew your understanding of God's rules.
(cloth)   ISBN 189201615X   **$16.95**

The Bible—God's Word for the Biblically-Inept™   *Larry Richards, Ph.D.*
An excellent book to start learning the entire Bible. Get the basics or the in-depth information you are seeking with this user-friendly overview. From Creation to Christ to the Millenium, learning the Bible has never been easier.
(trade paper)   ISBN 0914984551   **$16.95**

Purchasing Information
www.starburstpublishers.com

Books are available from your favorite bookstore, either from current stock or special order. To assist bookstores in locating your selection be sure to give title, author, and ISBN#. If unable to purchase from the bookstores you may order directly from STARBURST PUBLISHERS. When ordering enclose full payment plus shipping and handling as follows: Post Office (4th Class)—$3.00 (Up to $20.00), $4.00 ($20.01–$50.00), 8% ($50.01 and Up); UPS—$4.50 (Up to $20.00), $6.00 ($20.01–$50.00), 12% ($50.01 and Up); Canada—$5.00 (Up to $35.00), 15% ($35.01 and Up); Overseas (Surface)—$5.00 (Up to $25.00), 20% ($25.01 and Up). Payment in U.S. Funds only. Please allow two to three weeks minimum (longer overseas) for delivery. Make checks payable to and mail to: STARBURST PUBLISHERS, P.O. Box 4123, LANCASTER, PA 17604. Credit card orders may also be placed by calling 1-800-441-1456 (credit card orders only), Mon-Fri, 8:30 A.M. to 5:30 P.M. Eastern Standard Time. Prices subject to change without notice. Catalog available for a 9 x 12 self-addressed envelope with 4 first-class stamps.